Clavichord
Discography

Clavichord
D i s c o g r a p h y

A comprehensive listing of recordings of the clavichord made between 1931-2020

Francis Knights

Peacock Press

Copyright © 2020

The right of Francis Knights to be identified as the Author of the Work has been asserted by him in accordance with the Copyright, Designs and Patents Act 1988.

All rights reserved. No part of this publication may be reproduced, stored in a retrieval system or transmitted in any form or by any means electronic, mechanical, photocopying, recording or otherwise, without the prior written permission of the author.

Published by Peacock Press,
Scout Bottom Farm, Mytholmroyd,
Hebden Bridge,
West Yorkshire
HX7 5JS,
United Kingdom

ISBN 978-1-912271-65-8

Designed by DM Design and Print

Cover image:
Clavichord by J. A. Hass, Hamburg, 1763, MIMEd 4322,
by permission of the University of Edinburgh

*In memory of John Parry (1930-2016),
in whose hands I first heard the clavichord*

Acknowledgements

My interest in clavichord recordings began at school, with the purchase of Colin Tilney's recent disc of Fantasias on Archiv, and Thurston Dart's 1961 L'Oiseau-Lyre LP of Bach's French Suites. A chance remark read in an article a decade later, to the effect that there were few clavichord recordings, and fewer still of quality, provoked me to start collecting information about these discs, and within a few years I had enough material to publish some twelve pages of listings in an article in the *Music Review* (1990). By then, the expansion of the recording industry caused by the CD was well underway, and the improvement in recording techniques meant that it was now relatively straightforward to capture the full range of the clavichord's delicate sonorities. Since then there has been a flood of clavichord discs, hardly diminished by the decline in the record industry during the past decade.

I have continued to collect data since that 1990 publication, with the assistance of many friends, colleagues and correspondents. Recordings have kindly been loaned or given by Peter Bavington, Richard Ireland, the late Rodger and Lynne Mirrey, the late Virginia Pleasants, Paul Simmonds, the late Clifford West and many others; I have benefited from bibliographical and other assistance from Lothar Bemmann, David Gutman and David Kelzenberg; numerous record companies have generously provided copies of discs; and many performers, including Bernard Brauchli, Timothy Broege, James Cook, the late Ruth Dyson, Renée Geoffrion, the late Michael Thomas, the late Denis Vaughan, Eilif Zachariassen and Jean-Claude Zehnder, helpfully provided me with their recordings. My thanks are also due to Koen Vermeij, founding Editor of *Clavichord International*, to the editors of the various review publications who allowed me to indulge my enthusiasm for clavichord recordings, and to colleagues at MCPS and King's College London where I spent many years professionally as a discographer.

Much of the initial research was undertaken at the former National Sound Archive, London, and in the Bodleian Library, Oxford, to whose staff I am very grateful; I was also supported by the award of an Edison Fellowship at the British Library in 2004. In the past decade or so, the Internet has proved an invaluable source of information (and misinformation); although a useful source for some hard-to-find historic recording transfers, the many live recordings of very variable quality on (for example) YouTube have not been catalogued here, as they do not exist in a permanent and archival form.

Francis Knights
Fitzwilliam College
Cambridge
August 2020
www.francisknights.co.uk

Contents

Acknowledgements	7
Introduction	11
Key	15
Discography	21
Notes	236
Composer Index	238
Historic Instruments Index	254
Bibliography	258

Introduction

The first clavichord sound recording ever made was Arnold Dolmetsch's 1931 performance of two Preludes & Fugues from Bach's *Well-Tempered Clavier* for the 'Columbia History of Music' series.[1] Since that date more than 250 performers have contributed to the representation of the instrument on disc, and the past few decades have seen the production of a number of superb recordings.

Early clavichord recordings were both technically challenging to make and commercially difficult to sell, and so often appeared as brief historical illustrations among wider collections. Recordings of the clavichord pioneers include Arnold Dolmetsch, Violet Gordon Woodhouse, Dorothy Swainson, Erwin Bodky, Fritz Neumeyer and Ruth Dyson, few of whom were full time professional recitalists in the modern sense. A later generation of clavichord specialists captured on disc included Joan Benson, Ralph Kirkpatrick, Thurston Dart, Michael Thomas and Rolf Junghanns, while professional keyboard players like Christopher Hogwood, Gustav Leonhardt and Igor Kipnis have themselves been succeeded by younger generations of performers including Paul Simmonds, Michael Tsalka, Menno Van Delft, Ilton Wjuniski, Jocelyne Cuiller, Terence Charlston and Julian Perkins. Other performers who have made a particularly substantial contribution to the clavichord's discography include René Clemenic, Colin Tilney, Bernard Brauchli, Richard Troeger, Miklós Spányi and Jaroslav Tůma.

Repertoire choices have demonstrated a predictable focus on major Baroque and Classical composers (Bach and his sons, Haydn and Mozart are all very well represented), but the earlier periods also have some strong coverage, in the music of Cabezón, Froberger, Pachelbel and others. One very welcome development of the past few years is the increasing number of CDs of Renaissance clavichord music, a core (if not precisely definable) part of the clavichord's repertoire. The most significant recording project in progress remains the complete cycle of the solo keyboard music of C.

P. E. Bach by Miklós Spányi on BIS, now within sight of completion.

Many of these repertoire choices are player driven (consider Bernard Brauchli's extensive discography of Iberian music), which has resulted in a remarkably wide variety of music being available: some 350 composers, ranging from the Middle Ages to the contemporary. For example, there are now three recordings of *Howells' Clavichord* (Ruth Dyson, Julian Perkins and Jaroslav Tůma), a key part of the 20th century repertoire. In addition to classical music, folk, pop and jazz are all present, including discs from leading players like Keith Jarrett and Oscar Peterson; these demonstrate that the clavichord can also be a fascinating and effective contemporary music or jazz instrument.[3]

One continuing use of the clavichord on record has been to document the sounds of instruments in museums and collections (see, for example, recordings by Florian Birsak, John Kitchen and Fritz Neumeyer), and the representation of historic clavichords is now impressive. There are more than 70, including no fewer than seven instruments by the Hass family, with the many examples from the Hubert, Lindholm and Schiedmayer workshops allowing comparison of different clavichords by the same maker.

The clavichord has likely always had a domestic accompaniment role, for a single voice or instrument (as mentioned by C. P. E. Bach), and modern recordings have made balancing this more straightforward, with good examples of clavichord continuo available from Lucy Carolan, Terence Charlston and Eva Maria Pollerus, among others.

As a result of increasing interest about the types of keyboard instruments available to 18th century composers, complete recordings have begun to restore the clavichord to its rightful place in history. For example, a good proportion of the complete Haydn recordings by Christine Schornsheim and Tom Beghin, and the complete Mozart recordings by Siegbert Rampe and Arthur Schoonderwoerd, feature clavichord, alongside fortepiano and harpsichord. The same has been true of mixed-instrument recordings of Bach's *Well-tempered Clavier*. Another promising development has been of well crafted single-composer collections, for example of Froberger (Johannes Maria Bogner and Terence Charlston) and Müthel (Pierre Goy, Nicole Hostettler and Menno Van Delft); the reputations of these two clavichord-friendly composers in particular have been enhanced through high-quality recordings.

A wide variety of clavichords can be heard on these many hundreds of recordings, from the smallest Medieval instrument to the largest 19th century Swedish type. Instrument survivals have not always matched the key repertoire, and choices for Tudor music and even J. S. Bach remain uncertain. In the opposite direction, some types of instrument well represented through survivals, such as the late 18th century Scandinavian clavichord, have not had their own particular repertoire explored sufficiently. The problem of matching instruments and repertoire is often evident in the discography listings, with a tendency to use clavichords rather later in date than the music itself. And C. P. E. Bach for one would doubtless have been bemused at the thought of the many discs of his music on Hass instruments, which he is known to have disliked, due to their additional 4' bass strings!

Recent welcome signs in the field have been the increased number of imaginative arrangements recorded; the exploration of the 19th century repertoire (Anna Maria McElwain has recorded Chopin, for example);[2] and the appearance of some of the more specialized instruments: the pedal clavichord has been recorded by Erik Van Bruggen, Joel Speerstra and Harald Vogel, Renée Geoffrion has demonstrated an electro-acoustic clavichord, and 'lost' instruments like the 'Mersenne' clavichord have been reconstructed and recorded (Terence Charlston).

The availability of high quality historic instruments and copies has nearly driven out the 'revival' clavichords by Dolmetsch, Goff and others which were used at the beginning of the instrument's recorded history.

In one respect this is a pity: these quiet, gentle-attack clavichords were and are viable musical instruments in their own right, unlike the 'revival' harpsichords of the same period, and their particular sound-world is needed for much of the 20th century repertoire, particularly British music. Howells, for example, is not really suited to an 18th century German clavichord.

There remains much interesting repertoire to explore in the future, with W. F. Bach, Böhm, Buxtehude, Fux, Graupner, Koželuch, Kuhnau and Telemann among those needing better coverage, to take just the Germanic tradition. Hopefully this and other music from the 16th to the 21st centuries will continue to engage emerging generations of clavichord players.

Key

The entries are indexed alphabetically by performer, cross-referenced where a duet is involved. A three-letter code based on the performer name is attached to each entry, with a letter suffix where there would otherwise be duplication; thus, Walter Thoene is THO and Michael Thomas is THOa. A number follows this, representing the chronology of the recordings, with a second letter suffix to indicate subsequent reissues or versions of the parent disc. Thereafter, the data is arranged in five further lines, indicating the following:

PERFORMER
Code number
> Title
> Music content
> Instrument
> Format, Label, recording and date
> Reviews

The performer's name is given in capitals, supplemented with the names of any additional ensemble performers.

The code number uniquely identifies each recording issue, with exceptions such as the Hänssler Bach Edition and the Brilliant Classics *Mozart - Complete Works* and *Bach Edition*, where several performers appear in the set.

The title is given in italics if it represents the actual cover title of the disc; otherwise, it is descriptive. An asterisk at the head indicates that the recording also includes non-clavichord items, which are not listed here. This is followed by the total disc or set timing, rounded to the minute.

The recording contents are normally given in the original order where known, in a standardized format. Composers are separated by semi-colons, and works by commas. Numerous errors and omissions in track listings have been corrected and work-list catalogue numbers standardized as far as possible (note that both Wq. and H numbers are used for C. P. E. Bach); minor keys are shown in lower case, with sharps and flats indicated '#' and 'b'.

The instrument maker, model and date are listed, with a Boalch 3 identifier for historic instruments where known. Where several clavichords appear on one disc, a superscript letter system is used to key this to the contents.

The format of the recording is preceded by the number of items in a set, where relevant. Formats can include CD, 78 [with size indication where known], LP, C [for cassette], DVD, Video and mp3 or other digital format. This is followed by the record label, series name (where relevant), number, recording date and (P) date. Thus '2 CD Hänssler 92.117, recorded 2000, (P) 2000' indicates a two-CD set issued by Hänssler with the number 92.117, recorded and published in 2000. (Where a date given by a secondary source gives no indication as to whether it is a recording or (P) date, it appears alone.) This is followed by a code in brackets indicating any relationship of the issue to a previous one. An 'r' indicates a reissue, 'm' a mono version, 's' a set relationship, 'USA' an American issue number, and 'v' an unspecified relationship. Thus, the [r/SPA 8] at the end of SPA 8a indicates that it is a reissue of material (which may be complete or partial) from SPA 8. Reissue dates can also be included.

The review field includes English language reviews only (see the abbreviations list below); these reviews are often a useful additional source of information about the repertoire, for example identifying incompletely cited works, and the date of an issue.

In each case, where information is unknown (some of this material being completely unobtainable), it has had to be omitted. In many cases, the only way of acquiring full information about a recording has been to purchase the disc, hence this has become a very expensive project over the years.

Due to the ever-changing nature of the record catalogues, and the fragmented international nature of the market, 'availability' is not always easy to determine, and label distributors and current catalogue status are therefore not given here. The second-hand market, including Amazon and ebay, is a useful source for some rare material.

Some of these recordings were made for demonstration, private, broadcast or other non-retail uses and were not distributed commercially through record dealers. As well as the radio, television or online broadcasts listed, others were made by Maggie Cole, Thurston Dart, Peter Dickinson, Ruth Dyson, Genoveva Gálvez, Eta Harich-Schneider, Susi Jeans, Ralph Kirkpatrick, Pastór de Lasala, Anna Maria McElwain, Colin Tilney, Richard Troeger, Fernando Valenti, Ryan Lane Whitney, Peter Williams, Robert Woolley and many others; a select number of these made for the BBC have been noted here where copies (either archival or off-air) are known to exist.

Reissue history is often a tricky matter, as is shown by the complex Dolmetsch and Kirkpatrick listings, and further refinements to the sequence may in future be possible; for example, single 78rpm discs now circulate which were once only available as part of a set, making the exact chronology difficult to determine.

A considerable number of recordings stated by record booklets, catalogues and reference works to include 'clavichord' are errors or mistranslations (usually of 'harpsichord'), and do not in fact include any clavichord recordings; such 'ghost' citations are not included here.

The great majority of entries below are of classical repertoire, but there are many significant examples of folk, jazz and pop performers using the clavichord; these have been included only when they are solo or with one or two other instruments, or significantly represented on a disc. The electronic sound-alike instrument made by Hohner called the Clavinet has also been widely used, but does not appear here.

Review citations

BBCMM	BBC Music Magazine
BCSN	BCS Newsletter
CCD	Classic CD
CI	Clavichord International
Con	Continuo
EHM	English Harpsichord Magazine
EM	Early Music
EMR	EM Review
EMT	Early Music Today
Fanf	Fanfare
Gram	Gramophone
HFM	Harpsichord and Fortepiano Magazine
HY	Haydn Yearbook
HFN	Hi-Fi News
ICD	International Clavichord Directory (second edition)
IRR	International record Review
MQ	Musical Quarterly
MT	Musical Times
OY	Organ Yearbook
PBG 1970	Penguin Bargain Guide
PGBCD 1998	Penguin Guide to Bargain Compact Discs (1998)
PGCD 1990	Penguin Guide to Compact Discs 1990
PGCD 1995	Penguin Guide to Compact Discs (1995/6 Yearbook)
PGCD 1999	Penguin Guide to Compact Discs (1999)
PGCD 1996	Penguin Guide to Compact Discs (1996)
PGCDC 1992	Penguin Guide to Compact Discs and Cassettes (1992)
PGCDY 2000/1	Penguin Guide to Compact Discs Yearbook 2000/1
PSRG 1975	Penguin Stereo record Guide (1975)
PSRG 1984	Penguin Stereo record Guide (1984)
PPR	Performance Practice Review
RG	The Record Guide (London, 1955)
RR	Records and recording

SR	Saturday Review
Tangents	Tangents (Boston Clavichord Society)

The Discography

POPPY ACKROYD (also violin, piano, prepared piano, harpsichord, spinet, harmonium)

ACK 1

Feathers (41')

Ackroyd: Taskin

Anon triple-fretted, Mirrey Collection

CD One Little Indian Records TPLP1406CD, recorded 2014, (P) 2017

ACK1a

LP One Little Indian Records TPLP1406

DEREK ADLAM

[see also CHRISTOPHER HOGWOOD]

ADL 1

J. S. Bach: Three-part Inventions No.10 in G BWV796, No.11 in g BWV797; C. P. E. Bach: Prussian Sonata No.2 in Bb H25, Allegro in G H338, Rondo in e H272, 'Abschied von meinem Silbermannischen Claviere'; Grotthuss: Rondo in C; C. P. E. Bach: Fantasia in Eb H278

Derek Adlam after Johann Adolph Hass 1763

[BBC Broadcast c.1980]

ADL 2

Johann Sebastian Bach, The Universal Musician - Masterworks for Clavichord (77')

J. S. Bach: Toccata in G BWV916, Capriccio sopra la lontananza del suo fratro dilettissimo BWV992, Prelude, Fugue and Allegro in Eb BWV998, Suite in e BWV996, Fantasia and Fugue in a BWV904, Prelude and Fughetta in e BWV900, Prelude and Fugue in b BWV923/951, Prelude and Fughetta in G BWV902

Derek Adlam 1982 after Johann Adolph Hass 1763

CD Guild GMCD 7232, recorded 2001, (P) 2001

EMR (Dec 2001) p.21, *BCSN* (Feb 2002) p.30, *CI* vi/1 (May 2002) p.26

ADL 3

Haydn: Acht Sauschneider müssen sein (69')

Haydn: Sonatas in D Hob.XVI:24, in F Hob.XVI:29, in b Hob.XVI:32, Capriccio in G on 'Acht Sauschneider müssen sein' Hob.XVII:I, Variations in D Hob.XVII:7, in F Hob.XVII:6

Derek Adlam 1982 after Johann Adolph Hass 1763

CD Guild GMCD 7260, recorded 2002, (P) 2003

CI viii/1 (May 2004) p.29

SUSAN ALEXANDER-MAX

ALE 1

Johann Christian Bach: Keyboard Sonatas, Op.5 (74')

J. C. Bach: Sonatas Op.5/1-6

Peter Bavington 2006 after Johann Jacob Bodechtel c.1785

CD Naxos 8.570476, recorded 2008, (P) 2011

BCSN (Jun 2011) p.20, *CI* (May 2012) p.28

GUSTAV AUZINGER and MARTINA SCHOBERSBERGER

AUZ 1

Dialoghi

Vanhal: Duettinos Nos.10, 20, 23-24

Martin Pühringer 2012 after Anon c18th

CD Fra Bernardo fb 1507153, recorded 2015, (P) 2015

VALDA AVELING

AVE 1

C. P. E. Bach: Andante in b; J. S. Bach: Prelude and Fugue in e, Two-part Invention No.6 in E BWV777; Blow: Theatre Tune; Byrd: Galliard; Croft: Ground in c; Dandrieu: La Lyre d'Orphée; Farnaby: Tower Hill; Howells: Hughes's Ballet (from *Lambert's Clavichord* Op. 41); Peerson: The Fall of the Leaf; Purcell: Sefauchi's Farewell; Scarlatti: Sonata in e K15; Zipoli: Largo in b

Thomas Goff

BBC Sound Archives 23340 (January 1957)

AVE 2

J. S. Bach: Two-part Invention No.14 in Bb BWV785, C. P. E. Bach: Poco Allegro, Fantasia in c; W. F. Bach: Polonaise in d F12/4, Sarabande in e; Graupner: Air and Gavotte; Kirnberger: Chaconne in D, Sarabande and Forlane; Muffat: Sarabande in e,

Air in Bb; Telemann: Bourrée in A, Air in G

Barthold Fritz 1751

LP BBC Sound Archives LP 28574 (March 1964)

ANTONIO BACIERO

BAC 1

Obras Completas de Antonio de Cabezón [Vol. 5]

Cabezón: Fabordon de 8° tono No. 2, Kyrie de 7° tono No. 4, Ave Maris Stella

Anon [German c.1600, German National Museum]

LP Hispavox S90.075, (P) 1978

MARIA LUISA BALDASSARI

BAL 1

Andrea Antico, Frottole Intabulate, Libro Primo, 1517 (58')

Antico: Non resta in questa valle, Chi non crede che al mondo el sol nutrisca

Paolo Zerbinatti after Urbino intarsia

CD Tactus TC 480101, recorded 2015, (P) 2017

R. BARNATT

BAR 1

*[Recital with spoken poems]
LP BBC Sound Archives LP 22810 (July 1955)

STEVE BARRELL

BARa 1

Haydn: Four Sonatas for Clavichord (74')

Haydn: Sonatas in D Hob.XVI:19, in c Hob.XVI:20, in c# Hob. XVI:36, in Eb Hob.XVI:38

Pehr Lindholm 1785 (3)

CD Globe GLO 5023, recorded 1989, (P) 1989

Fanf xiii/4 (Mar/Apr 1990) p.192

BARa 2

W. F. Bach: The Complete Polonaises (61')

W. F. Bach: 12 Polonaises F12, Polonaise in C F13

Pehr Lindholm 1785 (3)

CD Globe GLO 5035, recorded 1989, (P) 1990

Gram (Sep 1990) p.566

OLIVIER BAUMONT

BAU 1

*Bach 2000: The Complete Bach Edition

J. S. Bach: Preludes in C BWV846a, in c BWV847a, in d BWV851a, in e BWV855a, Menuets in G and g BWV841-3, Wer nur den lieben Gott BWV691

Anthony Sidey 1995 after 18th century German models

153 CD Teldec 3984257042, recorded 1998, (P) 1999

BAU 1a

Bach 2000: The Complete Bach Edition [omitting sacred cantatas]

93 CD Teldec 3984257052 [r/BAU 1]

BAU 1b

Bach à la française

CD Erato 8573-80224-2, (P) 2000 [r/BAU 1]

IRR (Jun 2000) p.70, *EMT* viii/5 (Oct/Nov 2000) p.28

PATRICK BEBELAAR (also piano)

BEB 1

Pantheon

Bebelaar: Patheon [with Fred Daehn, Michel Godard, Herbert Joos, Frank Kroll, Carlo Rizzo]

CD dml-records CD 025, recorded 2005, (P) 2007

TOM BEGHIN

BEG 1

Carl Philipp Emanuel Bach: Pièces de caractère (69')

C. P. E. Bach: La Gause Wq.117/37, La Pott Wq.117/18, La Borchward Wq.117/17, La Böhmer Wq.117/26, La Philippine Wq.117/34, La Gabriel Wq.117/35, La Caroline Wq.117/39, La Prinzette Wq.117/21, L'Aly Rupalich Wq.117/27, La Gleim

Wq.117/19, La Stahl Wq.117/25, La Bergius Wq.117/20, La Buchholtz Wq.117/24, L'Hermann Wq.117/23, La Capricieuse Wq.117/33, La Complaisante 28, Les Languers tendres Wq.117/30, La Journaliere Wq.117/32, L'Irresoluë Wq.117/31, La Louise Wq.117/36, La Xenophon et la Sybille Wq.117/29, La Sophie Wq.117/40,[a] L'Ernestine I[a] Wq.117/16, L'Ernestine II Wq.117/38, L'Auguste Wq.117/22 [Jan van Elsacker, [a]tenor]

Joris Potvlieghe 2001 after Saxon models c.1760

CD Eufoda 1347, recorded 2002, (P) 2003

BCSN (June 2004) p.17, *CI* viii/2 (Nov 2004) p.57, *EM* xxxiii/2 (May 2005) p.355

BEG 2

**The Virtual Haydn: Complete Works for Solo Keyboard* (1001')

Haydn: Sonatas in C Hob.XVI:1, in G Hob.XVI:6, in C Hob.XVI:10, in E Hob.XVI:13, in D Hob.XVI:19, in Eb Hob.XVI:45, in Ab Hob.XVI:46, in e Hob.XVI:47, in G Hob.XVI:G1, in D Hob.XVII:D1

Martin Puhringer 2003 after Saxon instruments c.1760

12 CD [+DVD] Naxos 8.501203, recorded 2008, (P) 2011

BEG 2a

4 CD [Blu-Ray version]

MICHAEL BEHRINGER

BEH 1

*Diminuito (58')

[with Rolf Lislevand and ensemble]

CD ECM 4763317, rec 2007/8, (P) 2009

PIETER-JAN BELDER

BEL 1

*Bach Edition

Attrib J. S. Bach: Menuet BWVAnh 121; C. P. E. Bach: March BWVAnh 122, Polonaise BWVAnh 123, March BWVAnh 124, Polonaise BWVAnh 125, Solo per il cembalo BWVAnh 129; Hasse: Polonaise BWVAnh 130

Cornelius Bom 1992 after Hass

160 CD Brilliant Classics 99697, recorded 1999, (P) 2000

BEL 1a

*Bach Edition volume 1: Orchestral Works/Chamber Music – Notenbüchlein für Anna Magdalena Bach

23 CD Brilliant Classics 99701 [r/BEL 1]

BEL 1b

*Notenbüchlein für Anna Magdalena Bach

CD Brilliant Classics 93098 [r/BEL 1]

BEL 2 [see also PEN 1]

*Mozart - Complete Works (12000')

J. C. Bach, Sonatas in D Op.5/2, in G Op.5/3, in Eb Op.5/4

Cornelius Bom 1992 after Hass

170 CD Brilliant Classics 92540, recorded 1970-2004, issued 2010

BEL 2a

> *Mozart Edition Vol.4*
>
> 11 CD Brilliant Classics 99720, recorded 2001 [r/BEL 2]

BEL 3

> *Carl Philipp Emanuel Bach Edition (1777')
>
> C. P. E. Bach: Prussian Sonatas No.1 in F H24, No.5 in C H28; *Sechs Clavier-Sonaten für Kenner und Liebhaber* (1779): Sonatas No.2 in F H130, No.5 in F H243, No.6 in G H187; *Clavier-Sonaten nebst einigen Rondos fürs Forte-Piano für Kenner und Liebhaber* (1780): Rondos No.1 in C H260, No.2 in D H261, Sonatas No.1 in G H246, No.3 in A H270; *Clavier-Sonaten und freie Fantasien nebst einigen Rondos fürs Forte-Piano für Kenner und Liebhaber* (1783): Sonatas No.1 in G H273, No.2 in e H288, Rondo No.2 in E H274, Fantasia No.2 in A H278; *Clavier-Sonaten und freie Fantasien nebst einigen Rondos fürs Forte-Piano für Kenner und Liebhaber* (1785): Sonata No.1 in e H281, Fantasia No.1 in F H279; *Clavier-Sonaten und freie Fantasien nebst einigen Rondos fürs Forte-Piano für Kenner und Liebhaber* (1787): Sonatas No.1 in D H286, No.2 in e H287, Fantasia No.1 in Bb H289
>
> Geert Karman 1990 after Friederici
>
> 30 CD Brilliant Classics 94640, (P) 2013

BEL 3a

> *Carl Philipp Emanuel Bach: Preussische und Württembergische Sonaten (178')
>
> C. P. E. Bach: Prussian Sonatas No.1 in F H24, No.5 in C H28
>
> Geert Karman 1990 after Friederici
>
> 3 CD Brilliant Classics 94320, recorded 2011, (P) 2012

BEL 3b

    *Carl Philipp Emanuel Bach: Sonaten für Kenner und Liebhaber

    C. P. E. Bach: *Sechs Clavier-Sonaten für Kenner und Liebhaber* (1779): Sonatas No.2 in F H130, No.5 in F H243, No.6 in G H187; *Clavier-Sonaten nebst einigen Rondos fürs Forte-Piano für Kenner und Liebhaber* (1780): Rondos No.1 in C H260, No.2 in D H261, Sonatas No.1 in G H246, No.3 in A H270; *Clavier-Sonaten und freie Fantasien nebst einigen Rondos fürs Forte-Piano für Kenner und Liebhaber* (1783): Sonatas No.1 in G H273, No.2 in e H288, Rondo No.2 in E H274, Fantasia No.2 in A H278; *Clavier-Sonaten und freie Fantasien nebst einigen Rondos fürs Forte-Piano für Kenner und Liebhaber* (1785): Sonata No.1 in e H281, Fantasia No.1 in F H279; *Clavier-Sonaten und freie Fantasien nebst einigen Rondos fürs Forte-Piano für Kenner und Liebhaber* (1787): Sonatas No.1 in D H286, No.2 in e H287, Fantasia No.1 in Bb H289

    Geert Karman 1990 after Friederici 1765

    5 CD Brilliant Classics 94486, recorded 2011, (P) 2012

    BCSN (Oct 2014) p.18

BEL 4

    *J. S. Bach: Kunst der Fuge (118')

    J. S. Bach: 4 Duets BWV802-5

    Geert Karman after Friederici

    2 CD Brilliant Classics 96035, recorded 2018, (P) 2019

JOAN BENSON

BEN 1

    Music for Clavichord (34')

Anon: Preambulum (Buxheim Orgelbuch); Perrichon: Volte (*Thesaurus Harmonicus*, 1603); Cabezón: Duuiensela (1578); Froberger: Tombeau de Monsieur Blancrocher; Fischer: Prelude, Chaconne (from Suite No.8, *Musikalisches Blumen-Buschlein*, 1698); C. P. E. Bach: Fantasia in f# H300; Grotthuss: Rondo in C

Thomas Goff, Jacob Verwolf

LP mono Repertoire RM 901, (P) 1962

SR (27 Apr 1963), *High Fidelity* (May 1963)

BEN 1a

Music for Clavichord (34')

LP Bridge Records S 2250, Golden Voice series [stereo r/BEN1]

BEN 2

*Music of C. P. E. Bach played on Early Piano and Clavichord

C. P. E. Bach: Fantasia in c H75iii, Adagio assai in bb H74ii, Allegro di molto in F H75i, Adagio affetuoso e sostenuto in Ab H75ii (from *Probestücke* Sonatas H70-75)

Jacob Verwolf 1970

LP Orion ORS 76223, (P) 1972

BEN 3

Haydn and Pasquini on Boston Museum of Fine Arts Clavichords

Haydn: Sonatas in c Hob.XVI:20, in Bb Hob.XVI:18, in g Hob.XVI:44; Pasquini: Partite sopra la Aria della Folia da Espagna, Allemanda in c, Bizzaria in d

Johann Christoph Georg Schiedmayer 1796, [attrib] Onesto Tosi 1568

LP Titanic Ti-96, (P) 1982

Fanf vi/4 (Mar/Apr 1983)

BEN 4

The Clavichord: Music of Johann Kuhnau and C. P. E. Bach (37')

Kuhnau: Biblical Sonata No.2, 'Saul cured by David through Music'; C. P. E. Bach: Rondo in Bb H367, Rondo in e H272, 'Abschied von meinem Silbermannischen Claviere', Fantasia in c H75iii

Jacob Verwolf 1970

LP [Early Music Institute, Indiana University] Focus 881, recorded 1986, (P) 1988

PPR iii/1 (Spring 1990) p.103

BEN 4a

C Focus 931 [f/BEN 4]

BEN 4b

CD Focus 931 [1993 r/BEN 4]

BEN 5

*Clavichord for Beginners (71' + 86')

Froberger: Tombeau de Monsieur Blancrocher;[a] C. P. E. Bach: Fantasia in f# H300;[b] Haydn: Sonata in g Hob.XVI:44;[c] W. F. Bach: Fantasia in e F21[d]

[a]Thomas Goff, [b]Jacobus Verwolf 1960, [c]Johann Christoph Georg Schiedmayer 1796, [d]Pehr Lindholm 1785

CD + DVD [demonstration], Joan Benson, *Clavichord for Beginners*, Indiana University Press (2014), recorded 1982 [r/ BEN 1, BEN 3]

BEN 6

The Joan Benson Collection (125')

W. F. Bach: Fantasia in e F21; Wagenseil: Bells in the Vatican in Rome; Haydn: Sonatas in Bb Hob.XVI:19, in g Hob.XVI:44; Polak: Coranto; Trabaci: Versi; Anon: Preambulum (Buxheim Orgelbuch); Perrichon: Volte (*Thesaurus Harmonicus*, 1603); Cabezón: Duuiensela (1578); Froberger: Tombeau de Monsieur Blancrocher; C. P. E. Bach: Fantasia in f# H300; Grotthuss: Rondo in C

2 CD Clavier Classics CC108, (P) 2018 [r/BEN 1a, BEN 2 etc]. The Polak and Trabaci are 1977 live recordings on Verwolf 1960

BCSN (Summer 2019) p.19

MICHELE BENUZZI

BENa 1

*Johann Wilhelm Hässler: Keyboard Sonatas (251')

Hässler: *Sechs Liechte Sonaten fürs Clavier* (1780), Sonatas No.1 in G, No.2 in A

Andrea Restelli 2015 after Christian Gottfried Friederici 1765

4 CD Brilliant Classics 95225, recorded 2015/6, (P) 2016

WALTER HEINZ BERNSTEIN

BER 1

Historische Meisterinstrumente: Harpsichord, Hammerflügel, Clavichord

Acanta 23-506, recorded 1976-77, (P) 1982

BER 2

Eine Hausmusik bei Bach (58')

J. S. Bach arr Bernstein: Siciliano (from Violin Sonata No.1 in g BWV1001iii)

Johann Jacob Donat 1700

CD Capriccio 10 031, recorded 1983, (P) 1984

Gram (Sep 1985) p.410

BER 3

J. S. Bach, Inventionen & Sinfonien (75')

J. S. Bach: 15 Two-part Inventions BWV772-786, 15 Three-part Sinfonias BWV787-801

[Renate Ammer 1985 after attrib Gottfried Silbermann]

CD [no label or catalogue number], recorded 1997, (P) 1997

ANDREAS BEURMANN

BEU 1

Historische Cembali, Spinette und Virginale (53')

Paumann: Mit ganzem Willen; Kolberg: Es hat ein Baur

German c.1730

CD Korting-Musikverlag 4.2424

BERNARD BILLETER

BIL 1

Sämtliche Werke für Tasteninstrumente von Johann Kaspar Kerll: Volume 1

Kerll: Ciaccona

Berhardt Edskes

Fretted clavichord by Bernhardt H. Edskes

CD Motette CD 12161, recorded 1996, (P) 1997

BIL 2

Sämtliche Werke für Tasteninstrumente von Johann Kaspar Kerll: Volume 2

Kerll: Suites in D, in F, in a, in G

Berhardt Edskes

CD Motette-Ursina CD 12171, recorded 1996, (P) 1997

FLORIAN BIRSAK

BIR 1

Der Salzburger Klang: Werke Salzburger Komponisten auf historischen Musikinstrumenten des Salzburger Museums Carolino Augusteum (66')

Mozart: Minuets in G K1e, in C K1f

Anon [ex-Nannerl Mozart]

CD SMCA 0695, recorded 1995, (P) 1995

BIR 2

> *Mozart: Andante in F K616
>
> Anon c.1775/85
>
> CD to accompany facsimile published by the Internationale Stiftung Mozarteum Salzburg (2008), recorded 2008

ERWIN BODKY

BOD 1

> *2,000 Years of Music*
>
> J. S. Bach: Sarabande, Gavotte (from French Suite No.5 in G BWV816)
>
> [Maendler]
>
> 10" 78 Decca *Gold Label Series* DX-106, (P) 1931

BOD 1b

> 10" 78 Parlophone R1027 (from 12 x 10" set R1016-1027, B37022-37033 and Parlophone 11) [USA r/BOD 1]

BOD 1c

> 78 Parlophone/Decca P525 [r/BOD 1]

BOD 1d

> 78 record 1019 [r/BOD 1]

BOD 2

> *Johann Kuhnau: Le Combat entre David et Goliath*

Kuhnau: Bublical Sonata No.1, 'The Fight between David and Goliath'

12" 78 Anthologie Sonore AS-5 (from set *Anthologie Sonore* Volume 1 of 10 x 12" discs), (P) 1934

Gram (Feb 1935)

BOD 3

C. P. E. Bach: Rondo in e H272, 'Abschied von meinem Silbermannischen Claviere'; J. S. Bach: Menuet in G [Peters Anhang No.2], Polonaise BWVAnh 123, March in D BWVAnh 127, Chorale, Minuet in F [BG XXXVI p.210]

[Maendler]

12" 78 Anthologie Sonore AS-24 (from set *Anthologie Sonore* Volume 3), (P) 1935

BOD 4

Music of the Baroque Era for Harpsichord and Clavichord

Pachelbel: Aria Sebaldina in f; Fischer: Prelude Chaconne (from Suite No.8, *Musikalisches Blumen-Buschlein*, 1698)

LP Unicorn UN 1002 , (P) 1954

JOHANNES MARIA BOGNER

BOG 1

Cristoforis Clavichord (54')

Bach: Toccata in e BWV914, Partita No.6 in e BWV930; Froberger: Suite in C

Thomas Vincent Glück after Cristofori

CD ORF CD 3154, recorded 2009, (P) 2012

BCSN (Feb 2013) p.23

BOG 2

Domenico Scarlatti: Sonatas (73')

Scarlatti: Sonatas in A K208-9; in f K184-5, 238-9; in d K32, 141; in C K132-3, 513; in D K119; in g K30; in Eb K193; in a K175

Thomas Vincent Glück after Cristofori

CD Fra bernardo fb 1513497, recorded 2015, (P) 2015

BCSN (Oct 2016) p.19

BOG 3

Froberger's Traces (54')

Froberger: Toccatas 1 in a, II in d, VI in a, Capriccio III in d, Canzona VI in a, Ricercar I in C, Fantasia sopra Sol, La Re, Partita 'Auf der mayerin', Suite XXX in a, Tombeau de M. Blancrocher

Thomas Vincent Glück [2007] after Cristofori

CD Fra bernardo fb 1703213, recorded 2016, (P) 2017

DAVID BOLTON

BOL 1

*From Ruckers to Taskin: David Bolton plays his six early keyboard kit instruments

Farnaby: A Toy; Peerson: The Fall of the Leaf

David Bolton

C [Bolton Harpsichords] DB 101

ANDREAS SCOTTY BÖTTCHER

BOT 1

*Jazzimprovisationen auf Historischen Tasteninstrumente

Sassman

CD Phonector, recorded 1997, (P) 2006

GOTTFRIED BÖTTGER

BOTa 1

*Frö-höliche Weinacht

CD accompanying book by Gottfried Böttger and Norbert Hoppermann, *Frö-höliche Weihnacht: Beswingtes zum Fest* (Gutersloher Verlaghaus, 2008)

BERNARD BRAUCHLI

BRA 1

The Renaissance Clavichord (45')

Anon: Estampie, Estampie (Retrouvé); Paumann: Mit ganczem Willen wünsch ich dir; Anon: Quant ien congneu à ma pensée; Newsidler: Der Zeuner tantz; Weck: Tancz der schwarcz knab; Kotter: Fantasia in Ut; Löffelholtz von Kolberg: Es het ein Baur sein freylein verlohen; Anon: My Lady Carey's Dompe, The short mesure off My Lady Wynkfylds Rownde; Byrd: Earl of Salisbury Pavan; Attaingnant: Basse dance (Saint Roch), Gaillarde, Branle Gay de Poitou; Dalza: Pavana alla Venetiana; Gardane (ed): Lodesana Gagliarda, Gamba Gagliarda; Milan: Pavana, Pavana; Cabezón: Himno a 3; Valente: La Romanesca con 5 Mutanze

Peter Kukelka 1975 after Anon Austrian or South German instruments from the second half of the 17th century

LP Titanic Ti-10, (P) 1977

OY x (1979) p.191, *EM* vii (1979) p.569, *MQ* lxv (1979) p.134

BRA 2

The Renaissance Clavichord II (48')

A. Gabrieli: Intonatione de Primo Tono, Intonatione de Secondo Tono; Aston: A Hornepype; Gascogne arr Attaingnant: Bone Jesu Dulcissime; Obrecht arr Attaingnant: Parce Domine; Valente: recorded ercata del Terzo Tono; Bull: Spanish Pavan; Cabezón: Pavana Italiana, Diferencias sobre el Canto Llano del Caballero; Coelho: Tiento de Oitavo Tom Natural; Bruna: Tiento Llano de Cuarto Tono; Nassarre: Tocata de Primer Tono

[attrib] Onesto Tosi 1568

LP Titanic Ti-27, (P) 1978

Gram (Nov 1982) p.607

BRA 3

Keyboard Sonatas of Padre Antonio Soler

Soler: Sonatas No.24 in d, No.95 in A, No.67 in D, No.52 in e, No.116 in G

Eckehardt Merzdorf after Manuel Carmo 1796

LP Titanic Ti-42, (P) 1979

EM ix (1981) p.403

BRA 4

Carlos Seixas: Nove Sonatas (49')

Seixas: Sonatas No.1 in C,[a] No.16 in c,[a] No.25 in d,[a] No.35 in e,[a]

No.43 in f,[a] No.49 in g,[a] No.68 in a,[a] No.15 in G,[b] No.16 in G[b]
[*Portugaliae Musica* editions of Seixas: '80 Sonatas' (1965),[a] '25 Sonatas' (1980)[b]]

Eckehardt Merzdorf 1978 after Manuel Carmo 1796

LP EMI 077-40569, (P) 1982

BRA 5

Portuguese Keyboard Music from the 1700s at the Clavichord

Carvalho: Sonata in D, Sonata in g; Sacramento: Sonata in d, Sonata in g; Santo Elias: Sonata in d, Sonata in Eb; Madre de Deus: Fugue in d; Bachixa: Sonata in D; Baldi: Mara de Retirada

Eckehardt Merzdorf after Manuel Carmo 1796

LP EMI 7497331, (P) 1984

BRA 6

Tekladurako XVIII. Mendeko Euskal Musika

Oxinaga: Intento in g, Fuga in g, Sonata en 5° tono; Larrañaga: Sonata de Clave; Egiguren: Concierto Airoso; Etxeberria: Sonata de 5° tono; Sostoa: Allegro; Albero: recorded ercata, Fuga eta Sonata in D, Sonatas No.11 in d, No.12 in D, No.28 in e, No.29 in E

Eckehardt Merzdorf after Manuel Carmo 1796

LP IZ 262 D, (P) [1985]

BRA 7

Keyboard Works of Carl Philipp Emanuel Bach (71')

C. P. E. Bach: Fantasia in f# H300,[a] Sonata in d H139,[b] Variations on 'Les Folies d'Espagne' H263,[a] Sonata in b H73,[b] Sonata in A H29,[b] Rondo in e H272, 'Abschied von meinem

Silbermannischen Claviere'[a]

[a]Eckehardt Merzdorf 1978 after Manuel Carmo 1796, [b]Clifford Boehmer after Christian Gottlob Hubert 1782

CD Titanic Ti-186, recorded 1990, (P) 1990

EM xxi/1 (Feb 1993) p.161

BRA 8

Carlos Seixas: Sonate per tastiera (79')

Seixas: Sonatas No.6 in C,[a] No.8 in C,[a] No.12 in c,[a] No.13 in c,[a] No.14 in c,[a] No.29 in d,[a] No.33 in Eb,[a] No.51 in g,[a] No.XXIII in a,[b] No.XXV in b[b][*Portugaliae Musica* editions of Seixas: '80 Sonatas',[a] 2/1980, '25 Sonatas',[b] 1980]

Eckehardt Merzdorf 1978 after Manuel Carmo 1796

CD Stradivarius STR 33544, recorded 1998, (P) 1999

BRA 9

*Nannerl's Notebook

Mozart: Andante in C K1a, Allegro in C K1b, Allegro in F K1c, Minuet in F K1d, Minuet in G K1e, Minuet in F K2, Allegro in Bb K3, Minuet in F K4, Minuet in F K5, Allegro in C K5a, Klavierstück in Bb K5b, Klavierstück in F K6, Minuet in D K94

Egidius Heyne 1781

CD Stradivarius Dulcimer STR 33547, recorded 1999, (P) 2003

IRR (Nov 2003) p.54

BRA 10

Música Portuguesa para teclado dos séculos XVI e XVII (60')

De Paiva: Tento no modo de Mi, III Tom; Carreira: Ave Maria a Quattro, Quarto Tento a Quatro em sol, Fantasia a Quatro de Iº Tom; Coelho: Tento de Primeiro Tom por Dê La Sol Ré, Tento do oitavo tom natural, Primeira Susana grosada a quatro sobre de cinco; Alvarado: Tento de VI Tom por Gessolreut; da Cruz: Verso de 8º Tom por d-sol-ré; de Araújo: Phantasia de quatro tom; Madre de Deus: Fuga em Ré Menor, Fuga em Lá Menor

Anon [Iberian] 2nd half 17th century

CD Dialogos D100001 2, recorded 2000, (P) 2005

CI ix/2 (Nov 2005) p.53

BRA 11

Antonio de Cabezón (1510-1566) and his Contemporaries (60')

Gascogne arr Attaingnant: Bone Jesu dulcissime, from Treze Motets;[a] Attaingnant: Basse danse, from Quatorze Galliardes (1531);[a] A. Gabrieli: Pass'e mezo antico;[a] Aston: A Hornepype;[a] Anon: My Lady Carey's dompe;[a] Byrd: The Earl of Salisbury's Pavan;[a] Cavazzoni: Canzon sopra Falt d'argens;[a] Valente: La Romanesca con cinque mutanze (1575);[a] Narvaez: Quatro diferencias sopra Guárdame las vacas (1538);[b] Carreira: Ave Maria a 4;[b] Cabezón: Himno s 3, Himno XIX 'Pange lingua IV', Diferencias sobra el canto llano del Caballero; Tiento del séptimo tono sobre Cum sancto spiritu, de la Misa Beata Virgine de Josquin Des Prés, Diferencias sobra la villancico ¿Quien te me enojó, Ysabel?, Pavana Italiana[b]

[a]Peter Kukelka 1981 after South German or Austrian c.1680, [b]Anon Portuguese second half of the 17th century

CD Musica Antiqua a Magnano/Dialogos MAM-CD 3, (P) 2010

BCSN (Jun 2011) p.23

BERNARD BRAUCHLI[a] and ESTEBAN ELIZONDO[b]

BRA 12

Antoni Soler: Six Concertos for Two Keyboard Instruments (59')

Soler: Concertos No.1 in C, No.2 in a

[a]Eckehart Merzdorf 1978 after Manuel Carmo 1796, [b]Eckehart Merzdorf 1984 after Manuel Carmo 1796

CD Titanic Ti-152, recorded 1984-1985, (P) 1987

Gram (Nov 1987) p.771, *HFM* iv/5 (Apr 1988) p.132, *OY* xx (1989) p.143

BRA 12a

C Titanic Ti-152 [f/BRE 1)

BRA 13

Eighteenth-Century Music for Two Keyboard Instruments

J. C. Bach: Sonata in C; Blanco: Concerto No.1 in G; Olivares: Verso de Oitavo Tono

Clifford Boehmer 1980 after Christian Gottlob Hubert 1782,[a] Eckehart Merzdorf 1978 after Manuel Carmo 1796[b]

CD Titanic Ti-185, recorded 1989, (P) 1990

CAROLE LEI BRECKENRIDGE

BRE 1

The Bach Family & The Clavichord (76')

J. S. Bach: Capriccio sopra la lontananza del suo fratro dilettissimo BWV992, Chromatic Fantasia and Fugue in d BWV903; C. P. E. Bach:

Sonata in Bb Wq.49/4; Freie fantaisie in f# Wq.67; J. C. Bach: Sonatas in c Op.17/2, in G Op.17/4

Paul Irvin after Christian Ernst Friederici 1765

CD Arabesque Records [no number], (P) 2018

CHRISTIAN BREMBREK

BREa 1

La Danza de los Poetas (64')

Sanz: Folia, La Caballeria de Napoles, Espanoleta, Villano, Canario (from *Instruccion de Musica* 1674); C. P. E. Bach: Variations on La Folia H263; Falla: Homenaje, pour le tombeau de Claude Debussy

Eckehardt Merzdorf 1995 after Johann Christoph Fleischer 1729

CD Arte Nova 74321 85298 2, recorded 2001, (P) 2002

EMR, lxxxv (Nov 2002) p.18

BREa 2

*Joseph Martin Kraus: Sämtliche Klavierwerke

Tema con variazioni, VB 193, 2 Neue kuriose Menuetten (Scherzenminuetten), VB 190, Swedish Dance (Svenska dans), VB 192

Eckehart Merzdorf [1995] after J. C. Fleischer 1729

CD, Musicaphon M 56881, rec 2005, (P) 2011

TIMOTHY BROEGE

BRO 1

New and old music for clavichord (70')

Howells: De la Mare's Pavan, Sir Hugh's Galliard (from *Lambert's Clavichord*); Harrison: Sonatas Nos.1 and 5 (from *Six Sonatas*); Persichetti: Sonatinas Nos.5 and 6; C. P. E. Bach: Sonatinas Nos.3 and 4 (*Sechs neue Clavier-Stücke*, Wq.63.9-10). La Gleim, Wq.117/19; Hovhaness: Dark River and Distant Bell; Woodman: Warde's Dump, Gagliarda for Emily and Kip; Kosinksi: Prisms; Broege: The Sad Pavane, Sonatas Nos.1 and 2 (from *Five Sonatas*), Fantasia for clavichord, Partita for clavichord, Paws for a moment

Carl Fudge 1985 after J. C. G. Schiedmayer 1796

CD Allaire [no number], recorded 2015, (P) [2016]

BCSN (Feb 2017) p.26

NORBERT BROGGINI

BROa 1

Collection Ad Libitum, Vol. 1: Clavicordes et pianos (56')

Anon, Chacona

Anon, Spanish c17th

CD Ad libitum, (P) 2018

RICHARD BURNETT

BUR 1

The Finchcocks Collection of Historic Keyboard Instruments (52')

J. S. Bach: Prelude in E BWV854 (from *Das Wohltemperirte Clavier* Book 1)

Georg Friedrich Schmahl 1807

LP Amon Ra SAR6, (P) 1982

EHM iii/3 (Oct 1982) p.51, *EM* xii (1984) p.283, *Gram* (Oct 1982) p.459, *Gram* (Jan 1989) p.1190

BUR 1a

C Amon Ra C-SAR6 [f/BUR 1]

BUR 1b

CD Amon Ra CD-SAR6 [f/BUR 1]

BUR 2

Company of Pianos (52')

C. P. E. Bach: Presto in c Wq.114/3

Georg Friedrich Schmahl 1807

CD accompanying book, Richard Burnett, *Company of Pianos* (Goudhurst, 2004)

JOHN BUTT

BUT 1

Johann Kuhnau: The Biblical Sonatas (72')

Kuhnau: Biblical Sonatas No.2, 'Saul cured by David through Music', No.5, 'Gideon, Saviour of Israel'

Gary Blaise 1991 after Christian Gottlob Hubert 1789

CD Harmonia Mundi HMU 90 7133, recorded 1994, (P) 1995

Gram (Mar 1996) p.71, *BBCMM* (Feb 1996) p.79, *EM*, xxiv/4 (Nov 1996) p.715

BUT 1a

> *Kuhnau: Keyboard Works* (136')
> 2 CD Harmonia Mundi 2907360/61 [2003 r/BUT 1]

ISABEL CALADO

CAL 1

> *Toccatas, Sonatas e Minuetos, Autores Portugueses do século XVIII* (51')
> Seixas: Toccatas in d, in c, in f, in g, Minuet in A; Baptista: Allegro in C, Andante in C, Andante Grazioso, Spirituoso in Bb, Andante in G, Andante Vivace in D; Jacinto: Toccata in D
> J. C. Neupert 2007
> CD trofa [no number], recorded 2016, (P) 2016

CAL 2

> *Carl Philipp Emanuel Bach: Probestücke* (57')
> C. P. E. Bach: 6 Sonatas H70-75
> J. C. Neupert 2007
> CD trofa [no number], recorded 2015, (P) 2019

RED CAMP [Lafayette Berry 'Red' Camp]

CAM 1

> *The New Clavichord* (31')
> Camp: Prelude for Twelve Fingers, Twofer atonement, The Bluesando, Wing and a prayer, Waltz in left field, Purdie diddle dido twee twee, Nagasaki, Slow slow blues, Alma llanera, Cocktails for two, Ghost of a chance, Loosiana piano

LP Cook 1133, recorded 1957

Details BSCN liv (Oct 2012), p.34

CAM 1a

The New Clavichord (31')

CD Smithsonian Folkways Archival COOK 1133, (P) 2006 [r/ CAM 1]

PABLO CANO

CAN 1

Le Siècle d'Or du Clavier Espagnol

Albato: 3 glosados; Cabezón: Ave Maris Stella, Tiento del primer tono, Dic nobis Maria, Himno a 3, Para quien criè yo caballos; Baptista: Condito alme; Palero: Mire Nero de Tarpeya, Paseabase el rey moro; Anon: Pues no me queréis hablar, Diferencias sobre el Conde Claros

Goble

LP Harmonia Mundi HM 1001, (P) 1978

Gram (Nov 1978) p.937, *HFN* (Dec 1978) p.165, *RR* (Oct 1978) p.96, *EM* vii (1979) p.569

LUCY CAROLAN

CAR 1

*Carl Philipp Emanel Bach: 5 Flute Sonatas (74')

C. P. E. Bach: Flute Sonata in G H509, Flute Sonata in C H515 [with Nancy Hadden (flute)]

Karin Richter 1986 after Christian Gottlob Hubert 1771

CD ASV Gaudeamus CDGAU 161, recorded 1996, (P) 1996
Gram (Jun 1997) p.74, *Tangents* v (Fall 1998), p.5, *PGCD 1999* p.35

LUCY CAROLAN and PETER WILLIAMS

CAR 2

W. A. Mozart: Music for 2 Harpsichords, Clavichord and Fortepiano
Mozart: Fugue in g K375e [duet version]
Johann Adolph Hass 1763 (1)
LP Edinburgh recording Company SCH 801, (P) 1980

CHIARA CATTINI

CAT 1

Giuseppe Sarti, Opera completa da camera e per Tastiera (414')
Sarti: Sinfonia in C, Sonata in D (Allegro)
Mario Buonoconto
6 CD Tactus TC 721950, recorded 2012, (P) 2013

CAROLE CERASI

CER 1

Haydn & the Arts of Variation (73')
Haydn: Sonata in D Hob.XVI/19
Karin Richter 1998 after Christian Gottlob Hubert 1771

CD Metronome MET CD 1085, recorded 2008, (P) 2009

BCSN (Jun 2010) p.29

CER 2

Treasures of the Empfindsamkeit (71')

C. P. E. Bach: Freie Fantasie in f# Wq.67, Sonata in e Wq.52/6, La Stahl Wq.117/25, L'Aly Rupalich Wq.117/27; Müthel: Arioso with 12 variations in c; Mozart: Adagio in b K540; Haydn: Sonata in c Hob.XVI/20

Christian Gotthelf Hoffman 1784

CD Metronome MET CD 1091, recorded 2013, (P) 2014

BCSN (Feb 2015) p.23, *EMR* (Jun 2014) p.41

PHILIPPE CHANEL

CHA 1

Clavichord Music (34')

Paumann: Mit ganszem Willen; Kotter: Preambulum in F; Senfl: Kei Lieb ohne Treu; Anon: Bassa Imperiale; Dalza: Tastar de corde, Pavana alla Venetiana; Bendusi: Desiderata, Cortesana Padoana; A. Gabrieli: Intonatione Primo Tono, Canzon Ariosa; Frescobaldi: Toccata No.2 (from Book 2); Cabanilles: Tiento No.12 de falsas; Narvaez: Quatro diferencias sobre Guardame las vacas; Milan: Pavana, Pavana; Sandrin arr Hernando de Cabezón: Dulce Memoriae; Hernando de Cabezón: Ave Maris Stella; Sweelinck: Est-ce Mars

Clifford Boehmer 1983 after Anon, South German 17th century

CD Gallo CD-545, (P) 1988

ICD p.8

TERENCE CHARLSTON

CHAa 1

*Early Keyboard Instruments (76')

Anon (Celle MS): Englische Nachtigal;[a] Sweelinck: Malle Sijmen;[a] C. P. E. Bach: Fantasia in C Wq.63/6[b]

[a]Anon German, late 17th century, [b]Dolmetsch 1925

CD to accompany book, Mimi S. Waitzman, *Early Keyboard Instruments: The Benton Fletcher Collection at Fenton House* (London 2003)

CHAa 2

La Chasse Royale (92')

Anon: Allemande in c 'fitt for the manicorde', Allemande in c

Karin Richter 1997 after Johann Jacob Donat c.1700

2 CD Deux-Elles DXL 1143, recorded 2009, (P) 2010

CHAa 3

Carl Philipp Emanuel Bach: Spiritual Songs (56')

C. P. E. Bach: Passionslied, Bitten, Prüfung am Abend, Abendlied, Busslied, Trost eines schwermütigen Christen (from *Herrn Professor Gellerts Geistliche Oden und Lieder* H686); Seyn oder Nicht-seyn, Phantasie; Über die Finsternis kurz vor dem Tode Jesu, Passionslied, Der Tag des Weltgerichts, Empfindungen in der Sommernacht, Der Frühling (from *Sturms geistliche Gesänge mit Melodien* H749/752) [with Norbert Meyn (tenor)]

Peter Bavington 2009 after J. J. Bodechtel c.1790

CD Toccata Classics TOCC 0248, recorded 2012, (P) 2014

BCSN (Oct 2014) p.16

CHAa 4

Mersenne's Clavichord (69')

Févin: Sancta Trinitas; Anon: Prélude sur chacun ton, Longtemps y a que je vis en espoire, Prélude, La Bounette, Canaries, Borree, Volte appellee la Marcielleze, Pavane de Aranda, Fantasie sur l'air de ma Bergerer, 4 Preludes, Bergamasca, Gavotte, Courante La Chabotte; attrib Blondeau: La Magdalena; Costeley: Fantasie; Gombert: Hors envyeux; attrib Gardane: Gamba Gagliarda, Moneghina Gagliarda; Megnier: Prelude; Cellier: Pavane; Raquet: Fantaisie; de La Barre: Tu crois, ô Beau Soleil; D'orléans: Praeludium, Volte; Sweelinck: Toccata in C SwWV282; Boësset: Hereux séjour de Partenisse; Pinel: Bransle Les Frondeurs; Scronx: Echo in F; D'anglebert: Prélude (Suite in d); Chambonnières: Sarabande in a; Louis Couperin: Duo; Gigault: recit à trois; Lebègue: Laissez paistre vos Bestes

Peter Bavington 2010 after illustration in Marin Mersenne, *Harmonie Universelle* (1636/7)

CD Divine Art DDA25134, recorded 2014, (P) 2015

BCSN (Feb 2016) p.27, *CI* (May 2016) p.23

CHAa 5

Froberger: Complete Fantasias and Canzonas (62')

Froberger: Fantasias Nos.1-6, Canzonas Nos.1-6 (*Libro Secondo*, 1649), Fantasia; attrib Froberger: Fantasia Duo

Andreas Hermert 2009 after Anon (c.1680-1700)

CD Divine Art dda 25204, recorded 2019, (P) 2020

ROMAN CHLADA

CHL 1

Toccate da Roma

Frescobaldi, Michelangelo Rossi

Thomas Glück 2003 after Urbino intarsia

CD Monalvo, rec 2012, (P) 2014

DANIEL CHORZEMPA

CHO 1

*J. S. Bach: Well Tempered Clavier Book I

J. S. Bach: Preludes and Fugues in C BWV846, in C# BWV848, in d BWV851, in eb BWV853, in e BWV855, in F# BWV858, in f# BWV859, in g BWV861, in Ab BWV862, in g# BWV863 (from *Das Wohltemperierte Klavier* Book 1)

Hieronymus Albrecht Hass 1742 (1)

2 LP Philips 6769 106, recorded 1982

Gram (Apr 1985) p.1244

CHO 1a

2 C Philips 7654 106 [f/CHO 1]

CHO 2

*J. S. Bach: Das Wohltemperierte Clavier I & II (275')

J. S. Bach: Preludes and Fugues in C BWV846, in C# BWV848, in d BWV851, in eb BWV853, in e BWV855, in F# BWV858, in f# BWV859, in g BWV861, in Ab BWV862, in g# BWV863 (from *Das Wohltemperierte Klavier* Book 1),[a] Preludes and Fugues in c# BWV873, in Eb BWV876, in f# BWV883 (from *Das*

Wohltemperierte Klavier Book 2)[b]

Hieronymus Albrecht Hass 1742 (1),[a] attrib Johann Heinrich Silbermann c.1775[b]

4 CD Philips 446 690-2 [includes r/CHO 1], recorded [a]1982, [b]1994, (P) 1997

Gram (Jan 1998) p.38, *PGCD 1999* p.64

SERGIO CIOMEI

CIO 1

*Italian Violin Sonatas (70')

Locatelli: Violin Sonata in d Op.6/12 [with Fabio Biondi (violin) and Europa Galante]

CD Virgin Classics 5 45588-2, recorded 2002, (P) 2003

IRR (July/August 2003) p.51

RENÉ CLEMENIC

CLE 1

Tabulatur des Clemens Hor (51')

Anon: Je ne scay Trium vocum; Senfl: Allein din huld; Anon: Anfang ist lieben; Senfl: Pacientiam muss ich han; Hofhaimer: Nach willen dein; Dietrich: Ein meydtlin eim ladin lag; Grieter: Verschütt' hab ich das habermuss, Herbey herbey was leffel sey; Hofhaimer: A du min trost; Josquin: Duo; Senfl: Mag ich unglück not widerstan; Attrib Zwingli: Herr nun heb den wagen; Adam: Ach Jupiter; Hofhaimer: Mein ainings A, Min hertzigs A; Anon: tens mes amys; Scaramella; Lay qui moy fay; Schwartz Knab

Peter Kukelka after Anon c.1540

CD Arte Nova 74321 39105 2, recorded 1995, (P) 1996

ICD p.9

CLE 1b

Meisterwerke Alte Musik

6 CD Arte Nova 74321 59201 2 [r/CLE 1]

CLE 2

**Georg von Pasterwiz : Baroque Organ and Harpsichord Music* (56')

Pasterwiz: 300 Themes and Versets, Op. 4: Nos. 80-82, 84, 89-90, 235-239, 241-242, 247-248, 250-255

CD Arte Nova 74321 51637 2, recorded 1997, (P) 1997

CLE 3

Early Gothic and Renaissance Masterworks, Vol.1 (123')

I: Antonio de Cabezón: Glosas, Tientos, Himnos, Diferencias. Cabezón: Tientos II, XVII, Tiento del sexto tono, Composiciones a dos partes, Intermedios para los Kyries de Nuestra Senora, Duos IV, V, Ave maris stella a 3, Ave maris stella con diferencias, Ave maris stella III, Diferencias sobre la Pavana Italian, Diferencias sobre el canto De quien teme enojo Isabel; Verdelot arr Cabezón: Ardenti mei suspiri, Ultimi mei suspiri; Crecquillon arr Cabezón: Prenez pitie; Mouton arr Cabezón: Quaeramus. **II: Josquin Desprez: Motetti intabulati.** Josquin arr Cabezón: Inviolata, Inviolata I-III, Benedicta es, Benedicta es I-III, Ave Maria, Stabat mater, Stabat mater I-II, Benedictus (from Missa L'homme armé)

Anon unfretted (Clemencic Collection)

2 CD Arte Nova 74321 92781 2, recorded 2002, (P) 2003

CI vii/2 (Nov 2003) p.57

CLE 4

Early Gothic and Renaissance Masterworks, Vol.2 (181')

I: Music of the Spanish Renaissance at the Court of Charles V: Luys Venegas de Henestrosa: *Libro de cifra nueva para tecla, harpa y vihuela* (1557). Anon: Sacris solemnis, Fantasia sobre fa, mi, ut, re, Fantasia XII, Fantasia XVII, Fantasia XVIII, Pange lingua, O gloriosa Domina, Fabordones llanos 1, 2, 4-6, 8-10, Fabordones glosados 1, 4, 5, 7-9, Tres I; Alberto: Tres IV glosado de Luys Alberto; Cabezón: Pange lingua; Jachet: Aspice Domine; Mouton: Quaeramus; Palero: Paseabase el rey moro; De Soto: Tiento XXIII; Ureda: Pange lingua. **II: From the Tablatures of the Basle Humanist Bonifacius Amerbach (1495-1562).** Agricola: Tota pulchra es; Attaingnant: Ayme souffre que je vous ame, Jay trop ayme, Je me plains fort; Buchner: Ach hülf mich leid; Constanz: Dantz Moss. Bencznauer; Hofhaimer: Nach willen din, Min einigs A, Zucht eer und lob; Isaac: In pace, Si dormiero; Kotter: Ad te clamamus, Anabolch in fa, En est iltz ung qui ayme, Fantasia in ut,; Harmonia in sol, O herre got begnade mich, Praeludium in fa, Praeludium in la, Proemium in re, Salve Regina, Uss tieffer noot schry ich zu dir; Weck: Spanyoeler tancz, Tancz der schwarcz knab. **III: Doulce memoire. Chansons, madrigals, songs, motets and preludes from the tablature of Matthäus Waissel (1540-1602).** Anon: Fantasias I, II, IV, Zarth freundtlichs M; Arcadelt: Quand'io pens'al martire; Clemens: Je prens engre; Drusina: Quanto e Madonna mia; Hollander: Dum transisset I, Dum transisset II; Lassus: Susanne ung jour, Veni in hortum meum; Pathie: D'amour me plains, Si pourti guardo; Phalèse: Praeambulum I, Praeambulum II; Sandrin: Doulce memoire; Senfl: Was wirt es doch; Sermisy: C'est a grand tort; Languir me fais; Le content est riche; Vecchi: Neapolitana, Neapolitana; Verdelot: Ave Jesu Christe

Anon unfretted (Clemencic Collection)

3 CD Arte Nova 74321 99053 2, recorded 2002, (P) 2003

BCSN (June 2004) p.19

MAGGIE COLE

COL 1

Scarlatti: Sonata in A K208

Dometsch

[BBC Broadcast 1997]

JAMES COOK

COO 1

James Cook plays Bach's Well-Tempered Clavier, Book 1 (111')

J. S. Bach: Preludes and Fugues in C BWV846, in c# BWV849, in d BWV851, in eb BWV853, in E BWV854, in F BWV856, in F# BWV858, in A BWV864, in B BWV868, in b BWV869 (from *Das Wohltemperierte Klavier* Book 1)

Owen Daly

2 CD [no label] C940311-1/2

JOHN CRANMER

CRA 1

Bach, Bartók, Haydn, Howells and Music from the Fitzwilliam Virginal Book, played on the EM Shop Clavichord

Anon: Praeludium (from Fitzwilliam Virginal Book), Corranto (FVB No.201), Praeludium (FVB No.25); J. S. Bach: Minuet in

G, Minuet, March in D, Prelude and Fugue in a BWV889 (from *Das Wohltemperirte Clavier* Book 2); Haydn: Sonata in C Hob. XVI:2; Bartók: Staccato, Change of Time (from *Mikrokosmos* Book 5); Howells: Lambert's Fireside, Fellowes's Delight, Hughes's Ballet (from *Lambert's Clavichord* Op.41)

Early Music Shop after Anon c.1740

C Early Music Shop [no catalogue number]

KATHLEEN CREES

CRE 1

A recital of Clavichord Music (No.1)

C. P. E. Bach: Fantasia in f# H300,[a] Rondo in e H272, 'Abschied von meinem Silbermannischen Claviere';[a] Grotthuss: Rondo in C;[a] Anon: The short measure of my Lady Wynkfield's Round,[a] A toy;[a] Richard Farnaby: Fain would I wed;[a] Peerson: The fall of the leaf;[a] Giles Farnaby: Giles Farnaby's Dream;[a] Pachelbel: Fantasia in g;[b] Gottlieb Muffat: Air (from Suite in Bb);[b] Gibbons: Fantasia of four parts;[b] Purcell: A new ground;[b] Giles Farnaby: Tell me, Daphne;[b] Scarlatti: Sonatas in A K322, in A K208[b]

John Morley [a]'Silbermann' model, [b]'C. P. E. Bach' model

LP Fanfare 6530, (P) 1971

CRE 2

Jonathan and the Magic Clavichord

LP to accompany book by Kathleen Crees, *Jonathan and the magic Clavichord. A children's story with music* (1974)

CRE 3

Music by Pachelbel, Zipoli, Peerson, Farnaby, Henry VIII

and Anon

BBC Broadcast c.1981

CRE 4

Tapestry

Crees: Tapestry, Love lies bleeding, The cats, Slumber song, Dragonfly, The spinner, The magic clavichord, Blue tarantella, Cymbeline, A fine morning, The glow worm, Silken dalliance, The lady vanishes, A funny tune, Prelude to autumn, Skipping rope, Romance for clavichord, Sprint, A simple story, Spanish dance

LP De Wolfe DWS/LP 3316 [production music disc], (P) 1975

CRE 5

J. S. Bach: Short Preludes BWV924-928, BWV930, BWV931, 6 Short Preludes BWV933-938, Prelude and Fugue in f# BWV883 (from *Das Wohltemperierte Klavier* Book 2)

BBC Broadcast 1981

CRE 6

Harpsichord

Trad arr Crees: Clavichord Musette, Little Adagio, Sicilienne Triste, Prelude in Miniature, Salzburg Minuet, Courtly Polonaise, Florentine Sonata

CD Josef Weinberger JWCD 2082 [production music disc], (P) 1995

JACK RICHARD CROSSAN

CRO 1

Bach Behind Bars

Neupert

LP Westminster Gold, 1973, recorded live

CRO 1

Keyboard Kaleidoscope

LP Westminster Gold, 1973

CRO 3

Keyboard Excursions

Crossan: Prismatic Rag, A Child's Prayer, Classical Rock; Rota: Speak softly; Bacharach: Raindrops; Bach: Jesu, Joy of Man's Desiring; Beethoven: Variations on theme, Ode to Joy

C Janus recording JAN 1105, recorded c.1990

ALAN CUCKSTON

CUC 1

Dodgson: Clavichord Suites No.1 in C, No.2 in Eb

[BBC Broadcast 1978]

JOCELYNE CUILLER

CUI 1

O süsser Clavichord! (64')

J. S. Bach: Aria variata BWV989,[a] Fantasia in a BWV922,[b] Suite in e BWV996;[b] C. P. E. Bach: Suite in e H66,[b] Fantasia No.2 in C H284,[a] Variations on La Folia H263[a]

[a]Émile Jobin after Christian Gottfried Friederici 1773, [b]Patrick Chevalier after Christian Gottlob Hubert 1785 [sic]

CD Fuga Libera FUG508, recorded 2004

CI ix/2 (Nov 2005) p.55

CUI 2

C. P. E. Bach: Rêveries pour Connaisseurs et Amateurs

C. P. E. Bach: Cantabile from Sonata in b Wq.55/3, Rondo in A Wq.58/1, Fantaisies in F Wq.59/5, in Bb Wq.61/3, Sonata in a Wq.65/33, Rondo in C Wq.56/1, Freie fantaisie in f# Wq.67, Rondo in e Wq.66, 'Abschied von meinem Silbermannischen Claviere'

Jean Tournay 2005 after Christian Gottfried Friederici 1773, Patrick Chevalier 1994 after Christian Gottlob Hubert 1785 [sic]

CD Fuga Libera FUG536, recorded 2007, (p) 2007

BCSN xliv (June 2009) p.21

CUI 3

C. P. E. Bach: Sonates pour Yukio (56')

C. P. E. Bach: Sonatas in d H128, in c H121, in g H42, in G H56, in d H53

Jean Tournay 2005 after Christian Gottfried Friederici 1773

CD Ligia 1 CD Lidi 0101236-11, recorded 2011, (p) 2011

CUI 4

C. P. E. Bach: Socrate, Hamlet, Colin, Collett...

Jean Tournay 2005 after Christian Gottfried Friederici 1773

CD Ligia 1 CD Lidi 0101236-13, (p) 2016

LAURENCE CUMMINGS

CUM 1

C. P. E. Bach: Sonates pour clavier et violin (72')

C. P. E. Bach: Arioso in A H535 [with Adrian Butterfield, violin]

Eckehardt Merzdorf after attrib Johann Heinrich Silbermann

CD Atma ACD 2 2313, recorded 2002, (p) 2003

ALAN CURTIS

CUR 1

Haydn: Complete Keyboard Sonatas, Vol.1 (78')

Haydn: Sonata in C Hob.XVI:21

CD Stradivarius/Dulcimer STR 33521

Gram (Feb 1999) p.73, *BBCMM* (Apr 1999) p.88

MARIE-ANNE DACHY and JULIEN WOLFS

DAC 1

For two to play (64')

Türk: Sonatines in C, in Eb

Jean Tournay 1999 after Friederici

CD Ligia Lidi 0101269-14, recorded 2013, (P) 2014

ALEXANDRE DANILEVSKI

DAN 1

Stylems: Italian music from the Trecento (58')

[with Ensemble Syntagma]

John Morley 1989

CD Challenge Classics CC72195, recorded 2007-2008, (P) 2008

THURSTON DART[4]

DAR 1

Masters of Early Keyboard Music, Volume 1

Anon: La Bounette, La Doune Cella, La Shy Myse (from the Mulliner Book); Anon: Allemande; Croft: Sarabande (from Suite No.4 in c)

Thomas Goff 1946

LP L'Oiseau-Lyre OL 50075, (P) 1954

Gram (May 1955) p.531

DAR 1a

Four Centuries of Music for Organ, Harpsichord and Clavichord

5 LP L'Oiseau-Lyre OLS 114-8, (P) 1971 [set/DAR 1]

DAR 2

Henry Purcell: Complete Keyboard Works, Volume 2

Purcell: A New Irish Tune Z646, Rigadoon in C Z653, Sefauchi's Farewell Z656, Minuet in d ZT688, Ground in c ZT681, Air in d ZT676; Croft: Ground (from Suite No.3 in c)

Thomas Goff

LP Argo RG 83, (P) 1958

DAR 2a

LP Spoken Arts 208 (USA/DAR 2)

DAR 3

J. S. Bach: French Suites (51')

J. S. Bach: French Suites Nos.1-6 BWV812-817

Thomas Goff 1950

LP L'Oiseau-Lyre SOL 60039, recorded 1961, (P) 1961

Gram (Feb 1962) p.412, *PSRG 1975* p.32

DAR 3a

LP L'Oiseau-Lyre OL 50208 (m/DAR 3)

DAR 3b

LP Decca *Serenata* SA 5 (1982) [r/DAR 3]

Gram (Feb 1982) p.1174, *PSRG 1984* p.40

DAR 3c

C Decca *Serenata* KSC 5 [f/DAR3b]

DAR 3d

**J. S. Bach: The New Complete Edition* (16880')

222 CD + DVD Deutsche Grammophon 479 8000, (P) 2018 [r/DAR 3, see also KIR 2k, KIR 3c, KIR 5c, KIR 6d]

DAR 4

    Froberger: Clavichord Music (56')

    Froberger: Le Tombeau de Monsieur Blancheroche, Suite No.10 in a, Lamentation for Ferdinand IV, Capriccio No.6, Suite No.14 in g, Allemande (from Suite No.20), Ricercar No.6 in c#, Lamentation for Ferdinand III, Suite No.19 in c, Fantasia No.2, Suite No.3 in G, Allemande (from Suite No.30), Suite No.7 in e

    Thomas Goff 1950

    LP L'Oiseau-Lyre SOL 60038, recorded 1961, (P) 1961

    Gram (Jan 1962) p.358, *PSRG 1975* p.395

DAR 4a

    LP L'Oiseau-Lyre OL 50207 (m/DAR 4)

DAR 5

    Illustrated talk on C. P. E. Bach

    Johann Nicolas Deckert 1792

    BBC Broadcast 1963

DAR 6

    Thurston Dart plays Bach French Suites & Purcell (65')

    J. S. Bach: French Suites Nos.1-6 BWV812-817; Purcell: A New Irish Tune Z646, Rigadoon in C Z653, Sefauchi's Farewell Z656, Minuet in d ZT688, Ground in c ZT681, Air in d ZT676; Croft: Ground (from Suite No.3 in c)

    Thomas Goff

    CD J. Martin Stafford JMSCD 4 [r/DAR 2, DAR 3], (P) 1998

    ICD p.9, *BBCMM* (Jan 1999) p.76, *MT* (Spring 1999) p.63, *EM*, xxvii/4 (Nov 1999) p.678, *OY* xxviii (1998/9) p.161, *HFM* x/I (Autumn 2002) p.41

DAR 7

Thurston Dart plays J. J. Froberger & Early English Pieces (66')

Froberger: Le Tombeau de Monsieur Blancheroche, Suite No.10 in a, Lamentation for Ferdinand IV, Capriccio No.6, Suite No.14 in g, Allemande (from Suite No.20), Ricercar No.6 in c#, Lamentation for Ferdinand III, Suite No.19 in c, Fantasia No.2, Suite No.3 in G, Allemande (from Suite No.30), Suite No.7 in e; Anon: La Bounette, La Doune Cella, La Shy Myse (Mulliner Book); Anon: Allemande; Croft: Sarabande (from Suite No.4 in c)

Thomas Goff

CD J. Martin Stafford JMSCD 5 [r/DAR 1, DAR 4], (P) 1998

ICD p.9, *BBCMM* (Jan 1999) p.76, *MT* (Spring 1999) p.63, *Goldberg* (1999), *EM*, xxvii/4 (Nov 1999) p.678, *OY* xxviii (1998/9) p.161, *HFM* x/I (Autumn 2002) p.41

ULRIKA DAVIDSSON

DAV 1

*Haydn Sonatas (78')

Haydn: Sonatas in D Hob.XVI:14, in Bb Hob.XVI:2

Joel Speerstra and Per-Anders Terning 2001 after Johann David Gerstenberg 1760

CD Loft LRCD-1109, recorded 2005, (P) 2009

BCSN (Jun 2013) p.28, *CI* (Nov 2012) p.55

ULRIKA DAVIDSSON and JOEL SPEERSTRA

DAV 2

J. S. Bach: Die Kunste der Fuge BWV1080
CD Musica Rediviva (forthcoming)

GIOVANNI DE CECCO

DEC 1

Concerti Veneziani (66')
Vivaldi, Marcello, arr Bach BWV972-976
Michele Chiaramida 2015 after attrib Johann Heinrich Silbermann c.1775
CD Bottega Discanta BDI 295, rec 2016, (P) 2016
BCSN 72 (Oct 2018) p.18

DEC 2

Mozart Sonatas Vol.1
Mozart: Sonatas 8 in a K310, 9 in D K311, 12 in F K332
Michele Chiaramida 2015 after attrib Johann Heinrich Silbermann c.1775
CD Da Vinci Classics C00032, recorded 2017, (P) 2017
BCSN 72 (Oct 2018) p.18

DEC 3

Mozart Sonatas Vol.2 (73')
Mozart: Sonatas 13 in Bb K333, 16 in C K545, 11 in A K331
Michele Chiaramida 2015 after attrib Johann Heinrich

Silbermann c.1775

CD Da Vinci Classics C00033, recorded 2017, (P) 2018

DEC 4

C.P.E. Bach: 6 concerti per il cembalo concertato (73')

Joris Potvlieghe 2018 after Saxon models c.1770

2 CD Da Vinci Classics C00156, (P) 2019

DEC 5

Mozart Sonatas Vol.3 (76')

Mozart: Sonatas 2 in F K280, 7 in C K309, 18 in D K576, Allegro in g K312

Joris Potvlieghe 2018 after Saxon models c.1770

CD Da Vinci Classics C00034, (P) 2019

DEC 6

Mozart Sonatas Vol.4 (72')

Mozart: Sonatas 1 in C K289, 3 in Bb K281, 5 in G K283

Joris Potvlieghe 2018 after Saxon models c.1770

CD Da Vinci Classics C00035, (P) 2020

RATKO DELORKO

DEL 1

*Die Geschichte des Klaviers

J. S. Bach: Prelude in eb, BWV853

Bartolomeo Cristofori 1719

CD-ROM New Classic Colours NCC 8007, recorded [1996], (P) 1996

AURÉLIEN DELAGE

DELa 1

Le petit livre d'Anna Magdalena Bach 1725 (68')

Minuets in Bb BWVAnh 118, in c BWVAnh 121, Polonaise in d BWVAnh 128, Prelude and Fugue in C BWV846 (from *Das Wohltemperierte Klavier* Book 1)

Philippe Humeau 1999

CD Bayard Musique 308 450.2, rec 2015, (P) 2015

FEDERICO DEL SORDO

DELb 1

Antegnati: 12 Ricercari (58')

Ercole Pasquini: Toccata; Pellegrini: Canzon 'La Serpentina'; Soderini: Canzon 'La Ducalina'

Michele Chiaramida after Praetorius c.1620

CD Brilliant Classics 95628, recorded 2017, (P) 2018

DELb 2

Bonelli: Complete Keyboard Music (55')

Bonelli: Canzone 'Urania', Canzone 'Artemisia'

Michele Chiaramida after Praetorius 1620

CD Brilliant Classics 95816, recorded 2018, (p) 2019

LYNDOL DESCANT (and *voice)

DES 1

Dave Brubeck's nocturnes (25')

Brubeck: Going to sleep, *Strange meadowlark, recorded uerdo (Remembrances), Audrey, Study in fourths, *I see Satie, Strange meadowlark, Joshua Redmond, Softly, William, softly, Choral, Five for ten small fingers, Memories of a Viennese park, Upstage rhumba

Edelan aluminium clavichord

CD Edelan [no number], (p) 2011

ANDREW DE MASI

DEM 1

Godfried-Willem Raes: 4 Others (64')

Raes: Partition

Joris Potvlieghe

CD Logos Publiek Domain LPD006

PREETHI DE SILVA

DES 1

*Carl Philipp Emanuel Bach: Six Collections of Sonatas, Free Fantasias and Rondos for Connoisseurs and Amateurs, First Collection, Wq.55 (77')

C. P. E. Bach: Sonata No.2 in F H130

Koen Vermeij 1990 after Christian Gottlob Hubert 1771

CD Centaur CRC 3279, recorded 1996, (P) 2013

STEVEN DEVINE

DEV 1

Bellows, Jacks & Tangents (72')

Agrell: Sonata No.4 in e

Pehr Lindholm & Henric Johan Söderström 1806

CD Finchcocks Press FPCD002, recorded 1998, (P) 1998

STEVEN DEVINE and DAVID WARD

DEV 2

From Two to Six

Hässler: Sonata No.1 in F (for three hands)

Pehr Lindholm & Henric Johan Söderström 1806

CD Finchcocks Press FPCD003

PETER DICKINSON

DIC 1

20th Century Clavichord

Hoddinott: Sonatina; Dickinson: 5 Diversions; Ellington arr Dickinson: Prelude to a kiss, Sophisticated Lady, It don't mean a thing

Hugh Gough c.1958

BBC Broadcast 1989

DIC 2

20th Century Clavichord

Ridout: Suite; Dickinson: Suite for the Centenary of Lord Berners; Ellington arr Dickinson: In a sentimental mood, Don't get around much anymore

Hugh Gough c.1958

BBC Broadcast 1989

DIC 3

Blue Clavichord (78')

Dickinson: Suite for the Centenary of Lord Berners, 5 Diversions; Ridout: Suite; Hoddinott: Sonatina, Op.18; Ellington arr Dickinson: In a sentimental mood, Don't get around much anymore, Prelude to a kiss, Sophisticated Lady, It don't mean a thing

Hugh Gough c.1957

CD Heritage HTGCD 259, recorded 1989, issued c.2012 [r/ DIC 1, DIC 2]

BCSN (Jun 2014) p.23

ARNOLD DOLMETSCH

DOL 1

Columbia History of Music II

J. S. Bach: Preludes and Fugues in C BWV846, in Bb BWV866 (from *Das Wohltemperierte Klavier* Book 1)

[Dolmetsch]

10" 78 Columbia DB 505, recorded 1931

DOL 2

J. S. Bach: Chromatic Fantasia in d BWV903;[b] Preludes and

Fugues in D BWV850, in d BWV851,[b] in e BWV855, in bb BWV867 (from *Das Wohltemperierte Klavier* Book 1), in C BWV870,[b] in G BWV884, in F BWV881,[ab] in Eb BWV876 (from Das *Wohltemperierte Klavier* Book 2)[b]

[Dolmetsch]

7 x 12" 78 Columbia '48 Society' C.Rox 60-66, recorded [a]1931, [b]1933

Gram (Apr 1933) p.434

DOL 2a

J. S. Bach: Chromatic Fantasia in d BWV903

12" 78 Columbia '48 Society' Rox 60 [S/DOL 2], recorded 1933

DOL 2b

J. S. Bach: Prelude and Fugue in C BWV870 (from *Das Wohltemperierte Klavier* Book 2)

12" 78 Columbia '48 Society' Rox 61 [S/DOL 2], recorded 1933

DOL 2c

J. S. Bach: Preludes and Fugues in d BWV851 (from *Das Wohltemperierte Klavier* Book 1), in G BWV884 (from *Das Wohltemperierte Klavier* Book 2)

12" 78 Columbia '48 Society' Rox 62 [S/DOL 2], recorded 1933

DOL 2d

J. S. Bach: Prelude and Fugue in bb BWV867 (from *Das Wohltemperierte Klavier* Book 1)

12" 78 Columbia '48 Society' Rox 63 [S/DOL 2]

DOL 2e

> J. S. Bach: Preludes and Fugues in D BWV850, in e BWV855 (from *Das Wohltemperierte Klavier* Book 1)
>
> 12" 78 Columbia '48 Society' Rox 64 [S/DOL 2]

DOL 2f

> J. S. Bach: *a*Prelude and *b*Fugue in F BWV881 (from *Das Wohltemperierte Klavier* Book 2)
>
> 12" 78 Columbia '48 Society' Rox 65 [S/DOL 2], recorded *a*1931, *b*1933

DOL 2g

> J. S. Bach: Prelude and Fugue in Eb BWV876 (from *Das Wohltemperierte Klavier* Book 2)
>
> 12" 78 Columbia '48 Society' Rox 66 [s/DOL 2], recorded 1933

DOL 2h

> J. S. Bach: Prelude in bb BWV867 (from *Das Wohltemperierte Klavier* Book 1)
>
> CD to accompany book by Martin Elste, *Meilensteine der Bach-Interpretation 1750-2000. Eine Werkgeschichte im Wandel* (Stuttgart, 1999) [r/DOL 2]

DOL 2i

> **Clavichord and Harpsichord Commemoration recital* (52')
>
> J. S. Bach: Chromatic Fantasia in d BWV903; Preludes and Fugues in C BWV846, in d BWV851 (from *Das Wohltemperierte Klavier* Book 1), in C BWV870, in F BWV881, Prelude in Eb BWV876 (from *Das Wohltemperierte Klavier* Book 2)

[Dolmetsch]

LP Dolmetsch Foundation ARC 1017 [1984 r/DOL 1,2]

EHM iii/7 (Oct 1984) p.141

DOL 2j

C Dolmetsch Foundation ARCT 1017 [f/DOL 2]

DOL 2k

CD Dolmetsch Foundation ARCD 1017 [f/DOL 2]

DOL 3

Byrd: Pavan and Galliard 'Earl of Salisbury'

78 short play 10" Dolmetsch DR4, (P) 1937

DOL 3a

Pioneer Early Music recordings – The Dolmetch Family, Volume 1 (71')

CD Lute Society/Dolmetsch LSDO001, issued 2004

ROLAND DOPFER

DOP 1

Claviermusik des Barock

Peter Weidtman 1724

CD Organum Ogm 261029, recorded 2005, (P) [2006]

OLIVER DRECHSEL

DRE 1

Neefe: 9 Sonatas; Beethoven: Sonata WoO 47/1

Neupert 1999 after W. H. Baethmann 1799

CD Musikverlag C. Dohr, DCD-026, recorded 2005, (P) 2006

STEPHEN DRURY

DRU 1

John Zorn: From Silence to Sorcery

John Zorn: From Silence to Sorcery [with Fred Sherry (cello), Jennifer Choi (violin), Lois Martin (viola), William Winant (percussion), Bradley Lubman (conductor)]

CD Tzadik 8035, (P) 2007

JEAN-JACQUES DÜNKI

DUN 1

*Tétraclavier (65')

Dünki: Tétraptéron 0-IV [with Paul Clemann (piano), Stéphane Reymond (harpsichord), Pierre Subiet (celesta)]

Gerrit Klop, 1981

CD Jecklin JS 289-2, recorded 1992, (P) 1993

DUN 2

*Pour le clavier (67')

Dünki: Andere kindestücke (1960-2002), Cinq études pour le clavichorde (1990-2012), Zwei studien (2004)

Thomas Steiner 2006 after Christian Gottlob Friederici 1773

CD Pianoversal PV 102, recorded 2013, (P) 2018

MATHIEU DUPOUY

DUP 1

Carl Philipp Emanuel Bach, Pensées nocturnes (60')

C. P. E. Bach: Fantasia I in F H279, Fantasia II in C H284, Sonata in e H106, Sonata I in e H281, Sonata in g H68, Fantasia in f# H300, 'C. P. E. Bachs Empfindungen', Abschied von meinem Silbemannischen Claviere, in einem Rondo H66

Martin Kather 2002 after Christian Gottlob Hubert 1787

CD Hérissons Production 02, recorded 2008, (P) 2009

BCSN (Jun 2010) p.21, *HFP* (Spring 2014) p.36

RUTH DYSON

DYS 1

Howells and the Clavichord

Howells: Lambert's Clavichord Op.41; Goff's Fireside, Patrick's Siciliano, Dyson's Delight, Ralph's Pavane and Galliard, Finzi's Rest, Berkeley's Rest, Walton's Toye (from *Howells' Clavichord*)

Thomas Goff 1934

LP Wealden Prestige WS 194, recorded 1981, (P) 1981

DYS 2

*The Dolmetsch Years, Volume 6

C. P. E. Bach: Variations on 'Les Folies d'Espagne' H263; Howells: Dyson's Delight, Hughes's Ballet (from *Lambert's Clavichord*); C. P. E. Bach: Fantasia in c H75iii [sleeve listing in error]

CD Pickwick PCD 1018, recorded live 1990, (P) 1992

DYS 2a

*The Dolmetsch Years, Volume 6

C Pickwick CIMPC 1018 [f/DYS 2]

DYS 2b

Video Black Dragon [video/DYS 2]

RUTH DYSON and PETER MEDHURST

DYS 3

For two to play (58')

Anon: Sonata à quatre mains; Shuster: La Savoyarde; Mozart arr Neefe: Petite piéce tiree de l'opera 'Il Flauto Magico'

Thomas Goff 1934

C Wealden Prestige WSC 244, recorded 1987

ANDREAS EDLUND

EDL 1

*Tugend und Untugend: German Secular Songs and Instrumental

Music from the Time of Luther (70')

Isaac arr Kleber: In meinem Sinn; Isaac arr Kotter: In meinem Sinn; Hofhaimer arr Kotter: Mein einigs A, Zucht, eer und lob

CD Naxos 8.553352, recorded 1994, (P) 1995

Gram (Jan 1996) p.97

ESTEBAN ELIZONDO

[see Bernard Brauchli]

PÉTER ELLA

ELL 1

Joseph Haydn: Divertimento-Sonaten (74')

Haydn: Divertimentos in C Hob.XVI:1, in D Hob.XVI:4, in Eb Hob.XVI:13, in A Hob.XVI:12, in D Hob.XVI:19, Partitas in Bb Hob.XVI:2, in G Hob.XVI:6

Martin Pühringer 1998 after anon late 18th century

CD Sound Express EPCD 990350, recorded 1999

CI iv/2 (Nov 2000) p.57, *ICD* p.9

ELL 2

*Hommage in D (76')

J. S. Bach: Chromatic Fantasia and Fugue in d BWV903, Sonata in D BWV964

Martin Pühringer 1999 after Johann Christian Georg Schiedmayer 1796

CD Sound Express EPCD 2250, recorded 2000

ELL 3

Sweelinck: Toccaten, Fantasien, Variationen (75')

Sweelinck: Praeludium Toccata, Chromatic Fantasia, Mein junges leben, Toccata in a, Lachrimae Pavan, Psalm 140, Fantasia, Echo Fantasia, Echo Fantasia, Unter der Linden grüne, Toccata in C, Est-ce Mars, Vater unser im Himmelreich

Martin Pühringer 2000 after Johann Jacob Donat 1700

CD Sound Express EPCD 02440, recorded 2001

BCSN (Feb 2003) p.14, *CI* vii/2 (Nov 2003) p.57

MARIA ERDMAN

ERD 1

Clavischordae Aetas Aurea in Polonia: The manuscript of the St. Clare cloister in Stary Sący, vol. 1 (57')

Anon: Pieces 1-19, 23-36

Franz Joseph Bouthillier 1790, Andreas Hermert 2004 after Georg Haase 1692, Ryszard Moroz 1979-87 after Anon 18th century, Andreas Hermert 2005 after Albertus Septemda 16[ ]4, Zygmunt Karczmarski 2000

CD Acte Préalabe APO 127, recorded 2004, (P) 2006

BCSN xxxix (Oct 2007) p.16, *CI* xii/1 (May 2008) p.40

ERD 2

Clavischordae Aetas Aurea in Polonia: The manuscript of the St. Clare cloister in Stary Sący, vol. 2 (62')

Anon: Pieces 37-69

Franz Joseph Bouthillier 1790, Andreas Hermert 2004 after Georg Haase 1692, Ryszard Moroz 1979-87 after Anon 18th century, Andreas Hermert 2005 after Albertus Septemda 16[ ]4, Zygmunt Karczmarski 2000

CD Acte Préalabe APO 128, recorded 2004, (P) 2006

BCSN xxxix (Oct 2007) p.16, *CI* xii/1 (May 2008) p.40

ERD 3

Clavischordae Aetas Aurea in Polonia: The manuscript of the St. Clare cloister in Stary Sący, vol. 3 (58')

Anon: Pieces 1-19, 23-36

Franz Joseph Bouthillier 1790, Andreas Hermert 2004 after Georg Haase 1692, Ryszard Moroz 1979-87 after Anon 18th century, Andreas Hermert 2005 after Albertus Septemda 16[ ]4, Zygmunt Karczmarski 2000

CD Acte Préalabe APO 129, recorded 2004, (P) 2006

BCSN xxxix (Oct 2007) p.16, *CI* xii/1 (May 2008) p.40

MARTIN FARRAR

FAR 1

Bach: The Art of Fugue (139')

J. S. Bach: The Art of Fugue BWV1080, Fantasia and Fugue in a BWV904, Fughetta super Dies sind die Heil'gen zehn gebot BWV679; Buxtehude: La Capricciosa; Scarlatti: Sonatas K2, 55, 70, 86, 172, 328, 345 and 397

Douglas Hollick 1979 after Hass 1763

2 CD [no label or number], recorded 2006

BCSN xl (Feb 2008) p.18, *CI* xii/1 (May 2008) p.39

ALAN FEN-TAYLOR

FEN 1

J. S. Bach: Preludes and Fugues in C BWV870, in c BWV871 (from *Das Wohltemperierte Klavier* Book 2), French Suites No.1 in d BWV812, No.2 in c BWV813

C [private tape, live]

CREMILDE ROSADO FERNANDES

[see also MACARIO SANTIAGO KASTNER]

FER 1

Lusitana Musica, III Opera Phonographice Edita A/1: Música de Tecla do século XVIII (54')

Seixas: Sonata in C, Sonatas and Minuets in c, a, d

Anon [?Portugal, early 18th century]

LP HMV [A Voz do dono] 065-40 377, recorded 1974, (P) 1975

FER 2

Carlos Seixas: Sonatas (64')

Seixas: Sonatas and Minuets in C, in D, in d, in a, in f, in c, in Bb, in d, in A, Minuet in a, Sonatas in a, in C, in Eb

David J. Way and Marc Ducornet 1988 after Christian Gottlob Hubert

CD Philips 438 394-2, recorded 1992, (P) 1992

RONALD FROST

FRO 1

J. S. Bach: Klavierübung Part 3 (128')

J. S. Bach: *Klavierübung* BWV669-689 (excerpts: BWV 672-675, 677, 679, 681, 683, 685, 687, 689)

Alexander Temple 1990 after attrib Johann Heinrich Silbermann c.1770

2 CD Dunelm DRD0190, recorded 2002

GENOVEVA GÁLVEZ

GAL 1

*LP Musical Heritage Society IU 3315H

JÓSZEF GÁT

GAT 1

*C. P. E. Bach: Sonata No.2 in F H130

Ammer

LP Qualiton LPX 1151, recorded 1963, (P) 1966

Hi-Fi News xviii (Aug 1968) pp.74,76

GAT 1a

LP Qualiton SLPX 1151 [USA/GAT 1]

GAT 1b

LP Hungaroton HLX 90032 [1972 r/GAT 1]

GAT 1c

    CD Hungaroton Echo Collection HRC 1991

    [1999 r/GAT 1]

GAT 2

    Carl Philipp Emanuel Bach: Pieces for Clavichord (47')

    C. P. E. Bach: Fantasia in C (*Kenner und Liebhaber* vol.5), Sonata in Bb (*Kenner und Liebhaber* vol.5), Sonata in G (*Kenner und Liebhaber* vol.1), Fantasia in C (*Kenner und Liebhaber* vol.6)

    Ammer

    LP Qualiton LPX 1305, (P) 1967

    H-Fi News xviii (Aug 1968) pp.74, 76

GAT 2a

    LP Qualiton SLPX 1305 (USA/GAT 2)

RENÉE GEOFFRION

GEO 1

    Récital de Clavicorde

    W. F. Bach, Poco Adagio from Sonata No. 6 in a; C. P. E. Bach, Sonata in c Wq.65/31, Sonata in G Wq.62/19; Haydn, Sonata in C Hob.XVI:21; Mozart, Modulierendes Praeludium K624, Fantasia in d K397

    Renée Geoffrion & Pierre Buffiére 2000 after Silbermann

    CD Una Corda [no number], recorded 2006, (P) 2006

GEO 2

Louis-Philippe Rivet, Extraits du Nomoi of the Great Olympian Divinities (18')

Rivet: The Nomos of Aphrodite, The Nomos of Hephaestus, The Nomos of Hermes, The Nomos of Dionysius, The Nomos of Hades, The Nomos of Zeus

Renée Geoffrion after Anon Austrian c18th

CD [no label or number], recorded 2009, (P) 2009

GEO 3

J. S. Bach: Les Variations Goldberg (57')

Bach: Goldberg Variations BWV988 [Duo Alliance contre Nature: Renée Geoffrion (electro-acoustic clavichord) and Louis-Philippe Rivet (electro-acoustic bass guitar)]

Renée Geoffrion electro-acoustic clavichord

CD [no label or number], recorded 2009, (P) 2009

LUTZ GERLACH

GER 1

*Liese rieselt der Schnee

Sperrhake

CD LGM, (P) 2010

GER 2

*Fragile: 22 Miniaturen für clavichord

Lutz Gerlach: Fragile

Sperrhake

CD LGM, (P) 2010

LORENZO GHIELMI

GHI 1

Über Johann Sebastian Bachs Leben, Kunst und Kunstwerke (63')

Vivaldi arr J. S. Bach: Concerto in F BWV978

Andrea Restelli after Christian Gottlob Hubert 1787

CD Winter & Winter 910 105-2, recorded 2003, (P) 2004

MIRELLA GIARDELLI

GIA 1

*Trio Sonatas (57')

Quantz: Trio Sonata in G [with the Ariosti Ensemble]

CD Adda 581076, recorded 1988, (P) 1989

Gram (Oct 1990)

BERNHARD GILITZER

GIL 1

Musikinstrumente aus den Sammlungen des Museums

C. P. E. Bach: Allegro No.6 in D, Wq.113/6 (*Kurze und leichte Clavierstücke mit veränderten Reprisen*, 1766)

Christian Gottlob Hubert 1782

CD Deutsches Museum 971126, accompanying book by

Hubert Henkel, *Musikinstrumente. Ein Begleitbuch zur Ausstellung mit mini-CD* (1988)

FRANZPETER GOEBELS

GOE 1

The Story of the Keyboard Instruments, volume 1 (35')
Froberger: Lamento on the Death of Ferdinand IV; C. P. E. Bach: Fantasia in c; J. S. Bach: Aria; Benary: 3 Miniatures
LP Folkways FM 3326, (P) 1962

GOE 1a

The Story of the Keyboard Instruments, Vol. 1 (35')
CD Smithsonian Folkways Archival FM 3326, (P) 2007
[r/GOE 1]

THOMAS GOFF

GOF 1

Violet Gordon Woodhouse - her playing of the clavichord [illustrated talk]
[BBC Broadcast 1968] [text in Douglas-Hume 1996, Appendix V]

VIOLET GORDON WOODHOUSE

GOR 1

Anon: Woe Betide my Weary Body (from the Strallock Manuscript); J. S. Bach: Prelude and Fugue in C BWV846 (from *Das Wohltempereirte Clavier* Book 1); Mendelssohn arr Woodhouse: Overture to a Midsummer Night's Dream [includes brief recorded interview with Lance Sieveking]

Thomas Goff

[BBC Broadcast 1940, part re-broadcast 1997]

GOR 2

Great Virtuosi of the Harpsichord, Volume III: Violet Gordon Woodhouse (78')

Anon: Woe Betide my Weary Body (from the Strallock Manuscript); J. S. Bach: Prelude and Fugue in C BWV846 (from *Das Wohltempeirte Clavier* Book 1) [includes brief recorded interview with Lance Sieveking]

Thomas Goff

CD Pearl GEMM CD 9242, recorded 1941

EM, xxv/3 (Aug 1997) p.515

PIERRE GOY

GOY 1

Claviers Mozartiens (78')

Mozart: Gigue in G K574, Fantasia in d K397, Rondo in D K485

Thomas F. Steiner 1996 after Christian Gottlob Hubert 1772

SACD Lyrinx LYR 2251, recorded 2006, (P) 2007

PIERRE GOY[a] and NICOLE HOSTETTLER[b]

GOY 2

Johann Gottfried Müthel: Ariosi, Sonaten, Duette (172')

Müthel: Arioso in G,[a] Arioso in c,[b] Sonatas in F,[a] in G,[b] in C,[a] Duettos in C, in Eb[ab]

Thomas F. Steiner 1993 and 1996 after Christian Gottlob Hubert 1772

3 CD Cantando 2016, recorded 2000

BCSN (Feb 2003) p.18, *CI* vii/1 (May 2003) p.24

HANS GOVERTS

GOV 1

*Carl Philipp Emanual Bach, Sonaten

C. P. E. Bach: Sonatas in f# (1763), in Bb (1761), in f (1753)

3 LP Armida HG 124/126

MAUDE GRATTON

GRA 1

*Wilhelm Friedemann Bach: Fantaisies – Sonatas – Fugues - Polonaises (65')

W. F. Bach: Polonaise No.8 in e, Fantaisie in c FKnv2

Martin Kather 1999 after German models

CD Mirare MIR 088, recorded 2008

BCSN (Oct 2009) p.23

ANDREA GREGORI

GRE 1

"Touching the Wall (13')

Julia Usher: Clavicle: A touch-piece for clavichord

Fretted clavichord by Florindo Gazzola 2000

DVD Primavera [no number], recorded 2007, © 2007

INGER GRUDIN-BRANDT/INGER GRUDIN

GRU 1

*J. S. Bach: Suites in a BWV818a, in Eb BWV819a

Martin Sassman after Christian Gottlob Hubert 1763

LP BIS-69, recorded 1976, (P) 1977

GRU 2

C. P. E. Bach: Werke für Fortepiano und Clavichord

C. P. E. Bach: Rondo in a H262, Sonata in A H270, Fantasias in C H284, F H279

Martin Sassman after Christian Gottlob Hubert 1763

LP BIS-142, recorded 1979, (P) 1980

Early Music Record Services (Oct 1980), *Fanf* (Jan/Feb 1981), *Arg* (Jul/Aug 1981), *HFN* (Oct 1980)

GRU 3

*Bach recital (76')

C. P. E. Bach: Rondo in a H262, Sonata in A H270, Fantasias in C H284, F H279; J. S. Bach: Suites in a BWV818a, in Eb

BWV819a

CD BIS CD-142 [r/GRU 1, GRU 2]

GRU 4

Stockholmsklaver (73')

Anon: Air de la Belle, Air de l'amour, Menuet pour Mr C.Lindström, Gavotte de Comte Logie, Polloness, Serra (from Matthias Silvius Svenonis MS, 1721);[a] Dubut: Courante;[a] Anon: Gavotte C'est l'amour,[a] Gavotte;[a] Roman: Suite No.3 in G;[a] Grenzer: Polonaise;[b] attrib Åhlström: Andante con moto;[b] Bark: Tempo di menuetto;[b] Seterholm: Quadrille;[b] Agrell: Sonata No.6 in g;[b] Lagerfeldt: Pastorale andantino;[b] Pleyel: Menuetto;[b] Collin: Mar and Variations;[b] Swensson: Polonaise[b]

[a]Gottlieb Rosenau 1778, [b]Pehr Lindholm 1799

CD Hurv KRCD-21, recorded 1997, (P) 1998

CI iii/1 (May 1998) p.28, *ICD* p.10

PAULETTE GRUNDEEN

[see RICHARD TROEGER]

LUCA GUGLIELMI

GUG 1

Baldassare Galuppi: Sonatas for Keyboard Instruments (77')

Galuppi: Sonatas in a, in c 'Passatempo al Cembalo'

Kerstin Schwarz 1999 after Johann Christoph Georg Schiedmayer 1782

CD Accent ACC 24227, recorded 2009, (P) 2009

GUG 2

The new Bach image: keyboard perspectives for the 21st century (61')

J. S. Bach: Sonata in g BWV1001, Partita in E BWV1006a, Partita in d BWV1005: Ciacona

Angelo Mondini 1989 after Christian Gottlob Hubert 1784

CD Stradivarius 33995, recorded 2002-11

GUG 3

Bach & the early pianoforte (67')

J. S. Bach: Sonata in a BWV1003

Angelo Mondini 1989 after Christian Gottlob Hubert 1784

CD Piano Classics PCL0062, recorded 2013

FRIEDRICH GULDA

GUL 1

*Message From G.

J. S. Bach: Chromatic Fantasia and Fugue in d, BWV903; Gulda: Aria, Version 1; Blues for Joe Venuti [clavichord and piano]; Gulda/Goethe/Anders: Besuch vom alten G. [bass and alto recorder, piano, clavichord, drum, with Ursula Anders]

LP MPS 0188.049, recorded live 1978, (P) 1979

GUL 2

*The complete musician

J. S. Bach, Gulda, Gillespie and Paparelli

Wittmayer

[?3] LP Amadeo, recorded 1977-78, (P) 1978

GUL 2a

    3 CD, Amadeo 472833/5 [2003 r/GUL 2]

GUL 3

    Tales of World Music

    [with Ursula Anders, Mounir Bashir, G. Rabl]

    [?2] LP, Amadeo, recorded 1979, (P) 1980

GUL 3a

    2 CD, Amadeo 9865951, [r/GUL 3. 2003]

GUL 4

    So what? Freidrich Gulda – A Portrait

    DVD Deutsche Grammophon 00440 073 4376, recorded 1981/1986/1989, (P) 2007

GUL 5

    The Stuttgart Solo Recitals 1966-1979 (439')

    [with Günther Rabl (bass) and Ursula Anders (percussion)]

    LP, SWR Music, (P) 1966–1979

GUL 5a

    7 CD SWR Music SWR19081CD, (P) 2019 [r/GUL 5]

GUL 6

    Bach Clavichord, The mono tapes (60')

    Bach: Preludes & Fugues in D BWV874, in B BWV892, in Ab BWV886, in e BWV879, in a BWV889, in b BWV893,

Chromatic Fantasia and Fugue in d, BWV903, English Suite No.2 in a BWV807

CD Berlin Classics 0301063BC, recorded 1978-79, (P) 2018

BCSN (Spring 2019) p.9

GISELA GUMZ

GUM 1

Clavichord Music (65')

Weckmann: Variations on 'Die lieblichen Blicke';[a] Reincken: Suite in G;[a] Matheson: Fugue in G,[b] Fughetta in c;[a] Handel: Suite in d HWV447,[b] Fugue in c HWV607,[a] Fugue in Bb HWV610;[b] C. P. E. Bach: Sonata in b H73,[a] Telemann: Fantasias in g TWV 33/17,[b] in g TWV 33/8,[b] C. P. E. Bach: Fantasia in C H284[a]

[a]Hieronymous Albrecht Hass 1742 (1), [b]Johann Christian Gerlach 1769

CD Hungaroton Antiqua HCD 31185, recorded 1986, (P) 1989

Fanf XIII/6 (Jul/Aug 1990) p.355, *ICD* p.10

GUM 1a

LP Hungaroton Antiqua SLPD 31164 [f/GUM 1]

GUM 2

*Hamburger Clavier-Musik der Barockzeit

Hieronymous Albrecht Hass 1742 (1)

CD Museum für Hamburger Geschichte [no number], recorded 2003, (P) 2008

ROSALIND HAAS

HAA 1

Frescobaldi (105')

Frescobaldi: Toccata per organo [with Peter Krams, organ]; Libro Primo: Tocatas I, II, XII; Libro Secondo: Toccatas I, IV, IX; Fiori musicale: Missa della Madonna - Toccata per l'elevatione, Missa della Domenica - Toccata, ricercar sopo il Credo, Toccata cromatica per l'elevatione, recorded, ricercar cromatica post il credo

Sperrhake 1984

2 CD www.rosalindehaas.com [no number], recorded 2009-12, (P) 2012

MARCIA HADJIMARKOS

HAD 1

Haydn: Sonatas Hob.XVI:20, 32, 41, 42, 44, 48

Thomas Steiner 1992 after Christian Gottlob Hubert 1772

CD ZigZag ZZT 990901, recorded 1993, (P) 1999

CI iv/1 (May 2000) p.28, *IRR* (Jul 2000) p.80, *BCSN* xvii (Jun 2000) p.19, *CCD* (Jul 2000) p.73

HAD 1a

Joseph Haydn: 6 Sonates pour Clavier (80')

Haydn: Sonata Hob.XVI:41

CD Diapason No.117 [2019 r/HAD 1],

HAD 2

Carl Philipp Emanuel Bach: Pièces de caractère, rondos et fantaisie (67')

C. P. E. Bach: Rondo No. 3 in si bemol majeur Wq.58, La Borchward Wq.117/17, La Pott Wq.117/18, La Gleim Wq.117/19, L'Auguste Wq.117/22, L'Hermann Wq.117/23, La Buchholtz Wq.117/24, La Böhmer Wq.117/26, Les Languers tendres Wq.117/30, La Capricieuse Wq.117/33

Thomas Steiner 1992 after Christian Gottlob Hubert 1772

CD ZigZag ZZT 020301, recorded 2001, (P) 2002

CI vi/1 (Nov 2002) p.58, *BCSN* (Feb 2003) p.16

AAPO HÄKKINEN

HAK 1

Haydn: The Seven Last Words (66')

Haydn: The Seven Last Words Hob.XX/1:C

Attrib Johann Heinrich Silbermann c.1775

CD Alba ABCD 251, recorded 2005, (P) 2008

BCSN xliv (June 2009) p.18

HAK 2

*J. S. Bach, Sonatas for flute and harpsichord (70')

Bach: Flute Sonata BWV1035 [with Paulina Fred, baroque flute]

Jiri Vykoukal 2010 after Schiedmayer 1796

CD Naxos 8.573376, recorded 2015, (P) 2016

BCSN (Jun 2017) p.26

GERALD HAMBITZER

HAM 1

Das Hubert Clavichord im Stadtmuseum Bayreuth

J. K. F. Fischer: Suite in d 'Uranie' (*Musikalischer Parnassus*); J. S. Bach: French Suite No.5 in G BWV816; C. P. E. Bach: Sonata in A, Wq.55/4 (*Sechs Sammlungen von Sonaten, freien Fantasien und Rondos für Kenner und Liebhaber*), Fantasia in c Wq.63/6iii (*Achtzehn Probestücken zu dem Versuch über die wahre Art das Clavier zu spielen*, 1753); Mozart: Sonata in Eb, K282

Christian Gottlob Hubert 1756

CD Concerto Bayreuth 16 014, recorded 1993, (P) 1994

FANNY REED HAMMOND

HAMa 1

*The Belle Skinner Collection of Old Musical Instruments

J. S. Bach: Prelude in C BWV846 (from *Das Wohltemperierte Klavier* Book 1); Handel: Largetto (from Concerto Grosso Op.6/12)

Christian Gotthelf Hoffman 1784 (1)

LP J7-OP-6793/4, (P) 1958

ETA HARICH-SCHNEIDER

HAR 1

Das Schaffen Johann Sebastian Bachs

J. S. Bach: 15 Two-part Inventions BWV772-786, 15 Three-part Sinfonias BWV787-801

Anon 18th Century

LP Deutsche Grammophon Archiv APM 14083, 1950

Gram (Oct 1960) p.221

HAR 1a

LP Polydor 13014-5 [r/HAR 1]

HAR 1b

J. S. Bach: 15 Two-part Inventions BWV772-786

LP Parlophone PV.3406-7 [r/HAR 1]

HAR 1c

J. S. Bach: 15 Three-part Sinfonias BWV787-801

LP Parlophone PV.3408-9 [r/HAR 1]

HAR 1d

J. S. Bach: 15 Three-part Sinfonias BWV787-801

LP CdM.LD 8005 [r/HAR 1c]

GERALD HENDRIE

HEN 1

Renaissance and Reformation: Renaissance Music

Farnaby: Giles Farnaby's Dream

Alec Hodsdon 1948

LP Open University [accompanying course units 17-19], [c.1972]

SIEBE HENSTRA

[see also MENNO VAN DELFT]

HENa 1

Matthias Weckman: Sämtliche Klavierwerke (73')

Weckman: Toccata in d, Suites in d, in a, Lucidor eins hütt dr schaf, Canzona in C, Partita on Die Lieblichen Blicke

Geert Karmann 1991

CD Ricercar 206682, recorded 1998, (P) 1999

HENa 1a

Matthias Weckman: Kammermusik - Klavierwerke (133')

2 CD RIC 282 [2008 r/HENa 1]

HENa 1b

Matthias Weckman: Complete Works (313')

5 CD Ricercar RIC 369, [2016], [r/HENa 1]

HENa 2

Clavichord Lié (54')

Kotter: Proemium in re;[a] Hofhaimer: Carmen;[a] Anon (Buxheim Orgelbuch): L'ardant désir, Ma doulce amour, Repetico;[a] Kuhnau: Biblical Sonata No.4, 'Gideon, the saviour of Israel';[b] Froberger: Suite No.2;[b] Fischer: Passacaglia;[b] J. S. Bach: French Suite No.5 in G BWV816[b]

[a]Martin Kather 1999 after Leipzig No.2, [b]Anon, early 18th century, Brussels M1619

CD Musée des Instruments de Musique [Brussels] MIM007,

recorded 2000-1, (P) 2002

CI vi/1 (Nov 2002) p.57

ROBERT HILL

HIL 1 [also PAY 1, VID 1]

*J. S. Bach 2000: The Millennium Edition

170 CD Hänssler, (P) 2000

HIL 2

*Bach as Teacher [Hänssler Bach Edition vol.107] (121')

J. S. Bach: Chromatic Fantasia in d BWV903a, Applicatio in C BWV994, 13 Short Preludes BWV924-931, 939-943, 6 Short Preludes BWV933-938, Fughetta in c BWV961, Fugue in C BWV952, Fantasia in c BWV919, Menuets in c BWV813a, Eb BWV815a, Preludes and Fughettas in C BWV870a, in d BWV899, Prelude in G BWV902, Suite in a BWV818

Keith Hill 1997 after Friederici c.1750

2 CD Hänssler 92.107, recorded 1999, (P) 1999

CCD, *Gram* (Jun 2000) p.88, *CI* iv/2 (Nov 2000) p.56, *ICD* p.10

HIL 3

*Original & Transcription [Hänssler Bach Edition vol.110] (141')

Reincken arr J. S. Bach: Sonata in C BWV966, Sonata in a BWV965 (first movement)

Keith Hill 1997 after Friederici c.1750

2 CD Hänssler 92.110, recorded 1999, (P) 2000

CCD (Aug 2000) p.67

HIL 4

Bach: Werke für Tasteninstrumente

J. S. Bach: Chromatic Fantasia in d BWV903a, Applicatio in C BWV994, 13 Short Preludes BWV924-931, 939-943, 6 Short Preludes BWV933-938, Fughetta in c BWV961, Fugue in C BWV952, Fantasia in c BWV919, Menuets in c BWV813a, in Eb BWV815a, Preludes and Fughettas in C BWV870a, in d BWV899, Prelude in G BWV902, Suite in a BWV818; Reincken arr J. S. Bach: Sonata in C BWV966, Sonata in a BWV965 (first movement)

Keith Hill 1997 after Friederici c.1750

4 CD Master Music 4203-2 92.107, (P) 2004 [r/HIL 2, HIL 3]

CHRISTOPHER HOGWOOD

HOG 1

Music for Ferdinand and Isabella of Spain

Santa Maria: Fantasia No.25

LP HMV CSD 3738, (P) 1973

HOG 2a

CD Testament SBT1251, (P) 2005 [r/HOG 1]

HOG 2

Instruments of the Middle Ages and Renaissance (109')

Paumann: Ellend du Hast

Christopher Nobbs after Anon 16th century

2 LP HMV SLS 988, (P) 1976

HOG 2a

 Instruments of the Middle Ages and Renaissance

 2 CD Virgin Veritas x2 385 8112, (P) 2007 [r/HOG 2]

HOG 2b

 The Art of the recorder

 2 CD Testament SBT21368, (P) 2005 [Paumann r/HOG 2]

HOG 3

 Carl Philip Emanuel Bach: 6 Sonatas & 6 Sonatinas (67')

 C. P. E. Bach: 6 Sonatinas H292-7, 6 Sonatas H70-75

 Johann Adolph Hass 1761 (4)

 LP L'Oiseau-Lyre DSLO 589, recorded 1980, (P) 1981

 Gram (Jul 1981) p.290, *PSRG* 1984 p.18, *HY* xiii (1982)

HOG 3a

 C L'Oiseau-Lyre [f/HOG 3]

HOG 3b

 Keyboard Music on Authentic Instruments

 C. P. E. Bach: Sonata No.2 in d H71

 LP DSLO 609 [r/HOG 3]

 Gram (May 1983), *PSRG* 1984 p.1298

HOG 3c

 C KDSLC 609 [f/HOG 3b]

HOG 3d

    CD L'Oiseau-Lyre 444 162-2 [r/HOG 3]

    PGCD 1995 p.11

HOG 4

    The Secret Bach (72')

    J. S. Bach: Chromatic Fantasia and Fugue in d BWV903a,[a] Adagio in G BWV968,[a] Fugue in g BWV1000,[a] Allemande in g BWV836,[b] Menuet BWV841,[b] Menuet BWV843,[b] Partita on *O Gott, du frommer Gott* BWV767;[c] J. S. Bach arr Mortensen: Partita in a BWV1004[a]

    [a]Johann Adolph Hass 1761 (4), [b]Johann Jacob Bodechtel c.1790, [c]Adlam Burnett 1979 after Georg Friedrich Schmahl 1807

    CD Metronome MET CD 1065, recorded 2001, (P) 2003

    BCSN (June 2004) p.15, *CI* viii/2 (Nov 2004) p.58, *EM* xxxiii/2 (May 2005) p.355

HOG 5

    The Secret Handel (99')

    Handel: Aria and variations in G HWV430/4a,[a] Fugue in c HWV620,[a] Suite in c HWV446 [with Derek Adlam],[ad] Minuets in A HWV545-547,[b] Water Music: Air, Bourrée and Hornpipe in F,[b] Air in Bb HWV469,[b] Concerto in G HWV487,[c] Air (Lentement) HWV467,[c] Andante in G HWV487,[c] Allemande in b HWV479,[b] Courante in b HWV489,[b] Jesu meine Freude HWV480,[b] Chaconne in G HWV435;[a] Handel, arr Muffat: Suite No.3 in d HWV428;[a] J. P. Kreiger: Aria and variations in Bb;[b] Zachow: Sarabande and Gigue in b[b]

    [a]Johann Adolph Hass 1761 (4), [b]Johann Jacob Bodechtel c.1790, [c]Johann Heinrich Gräbner 1761 and [d]Derek Adlam 1982 after

Johann Adolph Hass 1763

2 CDs Metronome MET CD 1060, recorded 2002, (P) 2005

BCSN (June 2006) p.14, *CI* x/2 (Nov 2006) p.59

HOG 6

The Secret Mozart (74')

Mozart: Allegro in g K312,[a] Andante & variations K501,[a] Minuetto in D/Trio da M. Stadler;[a] Marche funebre K453a,[b] Andantino K236,[b] Klavierstück in F K33b,[b] Adagio for glass harmonica K356,[b] Lasst uns mit geschlungen Händen K623,[b] Rondo in F K494;[b] Theme & variations in A K460,[c] Fantasia in d K397 (two versions),[c] Sonata in D K381[cd] [with Derek Adlam]

[a]Johann Adolph Hass 1761 (4), [b]Anon, second half of the 18th century [ex-Mozart], [c]Johann Christoph Georg Schiedmayer 1791, [d]Derek Adlam 1982 after Johann Adolph Hass 1763

CD Deutsche Harmonia Mundi 82876832882, recorded 2004, (P) 2006

BCSN xxxvii (Feb 2007) p.25, *CI* xi/1 (May 2007) p.30

[a]CHRISTOPHER HOGWOOD and [b]CHRISTOPH ROUSSET

HOG 7

*J. S. Bach: Concertos & Duets (66')

W. F. Bach: Concerto in F F10; C. P. E. Bach: 4 Duets H610-613

[a]Johann Adolph Hass 1761 (4), [b]Johann Adolph Hass 1763 (2)

CD L'Oiseau-Lyre 440 649-2, recorded 1993, (P) 1996

Gram (Aug 1996) p.68, *HFM* v/1 (May 1997) p.31

CRISTIANO HOLTZ

HOL 1

J. S. Bach: Inventions & Sinfonias

J. S. Bach: 15 Two-part Inventions BWV772-786, 15 Three-part Sinfonias BWV787-801; Prelude in c BWV999, Fughetta in c BWV961, Preambulum in g BWV930, Minuet in c BWV813, Sarabande in F BWV823

Joop Klinkhamer after attrib Johann Heinrich Silbermann c.1775

CD Editions Hortus 052, recorded 2008, (P) 2008

BCSN xliv (June 2009) p.23

HOL 2

Carl Philipp Emanuel Bach: Sur le Véritable art de jouer les instruments à clavier (78')

C. P. E. Bach: Sonatas No.1 H70, No.2 H71 (*Achtzehn Probe-Stüke*), Sonata No.2 H295 (*Sonatine nuove*)

Geert Karman 1990 after Christian Gottlob Friederici 1765

CD Editions Hortus 052, recorded 2013, (P) 2013

NICOLE HOSTETTLER

[see also PIERRE GOY]

HOS 1

Johann Sebastian Bach: Die Kunste der Fuge (79')

J. S. Bach: Die Kunste der Fuge BWV1080

Thomas Steiner 1993 after Christian Gottlob Hubert 1772

CD Cantando 2019, rec 2009

BCSN (Oct 2010)

EDGAR HUNT

HUN 1

*[Demonstration of the Clavichord]

J. S. Bach: Prelude in C BWV846 (*Das Wohltemperierte Klavier* Book 1) (excerpt)

Anon 17th-century (Benton Fletcher Collection)

LP BBC Sound Archives LP 13719

SUSAN HURLEY

HUR 1

Soft Sounds

Hurley: Leaves, Edges, Earth, Sunlight, Blue, Metal, Images, Night, Saffron, Water

Jeffrey Resnick, fretted after Anon Swedish

CD Susan Hurley [no number], recorded 2004, (P) 2005

JOHAN HUYS

HUY 1

*Keyboard improvisations

Joris Potvlieghe

CD Stichting Logos, Publiek Domein LPD 010, recorded live 1995/2003

JOS VAN IMMERSEEL

IMM 1

Les claviers d'A.G. Musée des instruments de musique

Anon: Brande Champanje, Almande de symmerman, Almande de La nonette, De frans galliard, Almande Brun Smeedelyn, Almande [from the Van Soldt MS]

Martin Kather 1999 after Anon c.1540 [Leipzig No.2]

CD Sabam MIM 001, recorded 1999, (P) 1999

JOHN IRVING

IRV 1

John Irving plays Mozart on the Hass clavichord (77')

Mozart: Fantasia in d K397, Sonatas in G K283, in C K330, in Bb K570, Andante in C K1a, Allegro in C K1b, Allegro in F K1c, Menuetto in F K1d, Menuetto in G K1e, Menuetto in C K1f, Menuetto in F K2, Allegretto in Bb K3, Menuett in F K5

Johann Adolph Hass 1763

CD sfz Music SFZM0612, recorded 2011, (P) 2012

BCSN (Oct 2013)

HERMANN ISERINGHAUSEN

ISE 1

C. P. E. Bach: Fantasia in C H284; J. S. Bach: 6 Preludes BWV933-938

LP Cantate 643302 [mono], 1962

Gram (Sep 1962) p.149, *RR* (Oct 1962) p.47

ISE 2

Clavichordmusik des 17. und 18. Jahrhunderts (52')

Froberger: Suite No.19 in c; Böhm: Prelude, Fugue and Postlude in g; J. S. Bach: Chromatic Fantasia and Fugue in d BWV903; C. P. E. Bach: Fantasia in f# H300; J.C.Bach: Sonata in c Op.17/2

Franz Lengemann

CD Dabringhaus und Grimm MDG L 3139, recorded 1983, (P) 1990

ICD p.11

KEITH JARRETT

JAR 1

The Book of Ways (101')

Jarrett: The Book of Ways *The Feeling of Strings*

Merzdorf

2 CD ECM 831 396-2 and 1344/45, recorded 1986, (P) 1987

ICD p.11

JAR 1a

2 LP ECM 831 396-1/2 [f/JAR 1]

JAR 1b

:rarum 1 – Keith Jarrett (155')

Jarrett: The Book of Ways Nos. 12, 14, 18

2 CD ECM rarum 4400141682 [r/JAR 1]

SUSI JEANS

JEA 1

The First International Congress of Organists (London, 1957)

Naváez: Diferencias sopra Guárdame las vacas; Speth: Partita diverse sopra La Spagnioletta

LP Mirrosonic Documentary recording Vol.5, 1958

JEA 1a

LP Miranda 1010 [USA/JEA 1]

GUNNAR JOHANSEN

JOH 1

*J. S. Bach: Complete Keyboard Works

J. S. Bach: 15 Two-part Inventions BWV772-786, 15 Three-part Sinfonias BWV787-801, Invention in C BWV772, Prelude [No.29 from Anna Magdalena Bach Book]

Sperrhake

43 LP/C Artist Direct, recorded 1958, 1961

GERAINT JONES

JON 1

The HMV Baroque Library 23: Music for Virginals,

Clavichord and Harpsichord

J. S. Bach: Prelude in G BWV902; C. P. E. Bach: Andante (from Sonata No.2 in F H130)

Barthold Fritz 1751

LP HMV HQS 1100, (P) 1967

PBG 1970 p.539

SHARONA JOSHUA

JOS 1

*The Bones of all men

Trad arr Pickett: Passo e mezo, Der mohren auftzugkh [with Philip Pickett and ensemble]

CD Hannibal HNCD 1416, (P) 1998

ROLF JUNGHANNS

JUN 1

Originalinstrumente: Tasteininstrumente Vol.2 (46')

J. S. Bach: Preludes and Fugues in C BWV846, in Bb BWV866 (from *Das Wohltemperirte Clavier* Book1), Capriccio sopra la lontananza del suo fratello dilettissimo BWV902, French Suite No.5 in G BWV816

Christian Gottlob Hubert 1772

LP Toccata FSM 53 619, recorded 1975, (P) 1975

Gram (Sep 1977) p.504

JUN 1a

    CD Adagio ADG 91619 [r/JUN 1]

JUN 1b

    Johann Sebastian Bach: Claviermusik

    CD FSM Adagio FCD 91 619, (P) 1991

JUN 2

    3 LP EK6.35521 Telefunken *Das Alte Werke* [s/JUN 1]

    Gram (Sep 1977) p.504, (Sep 1981) p.418

JUN 3

    Original Instruments: Clavichord (43')

    J. C. F. Bach: Sonatina in a HWX.XII:13 (*Musikalische Nebenstunden*, 1787/88); C. P. E. Bach: Sonatas in F H243 (*Kenner und Leibhaber* I, 1779), in b H245 (*Kenner und Leibhaber* I, 1779); W. F. Bach: Sonata in Bb F9

    attrib Carl Christian Schmahl, end of 18th century

    LP Telefunken *Das Alte Werke* AP6.42073, (P) 1979

    Gram (Sep 1981) p.406

JUN 3a

    C Telefunken *Das Alte Werke* 4.42073 CR [f/JUN 3]

JUN 3b

    Originalinstrumente

    12 LP Telefunken 6.35488 [s/JUN 3]

HANNS KANN

KAN 1

The Sound of Keyboard Instruments

C. P. E. Bach: Rondo in e H272, 'Abschied von meinem Silbermannischen Claviere'; Anon: Pavanne Angloise in A; W. F. Bach: Polonaise No.4 in d F12iv

Neupert 1963

LP Musical Heritage Society MHS 862, 1967

KAN 2

History of Baroque Music

J. S. Bach: Duet No.1 in e BWV802; Prelude in Eb BWV852 (from *Das Wohltemperierte Klavier* Book 1)

Neupert

LP Orpheus OR 331, 1967

KAN 3

Early European Music for Clavichord (45')

Cabezón: Himno a 3; Narvaez: Quatro Diferencias sobre 'Guárdame las vacas' (1538); Santa Maria: Fantasia Primi Toni, Exemplo de quanto solamente se mudan las vozes intermedias; Cabezón: Otras Diferencias sobre 'Guárdame las vacas'; Attaingnant: Basse danse, Galliard; Denis Gaultier: Tombeau de M. de l'Enclos; Facoli: Aria della Marcheta Saporita, Tedesca dita l'Austria (1588); Dalza: Pavana alla Veneziana; Bendusi: Desiderata, Cortesana Padoana; Picchi: German Dance, Polish Dance; Valente: Il Ballo dell'Intorcia; Anon: Pastyme, In winter's just return, The Duke of Somerset's Dompe, The Duke of Milan's Dump, Pretty Ways, Pavanne Angloise; Paumann: Mit ganzem

Willen; Kindermann: Praeambulum undecimi et duodecimi toni; Noermiger: Ein ander Intrada, Der Mohren Aufzug; Weck: Spanyöler Tanz; Anon: Martin Again, Douce Memoir (Lublin Tablature), A good Polish Dance (Loeffelholz Tablature)

Peter Kukelka after 17th century model

LP Musical Heritage Society MHS 926, 1968

BÁLINT KAROSI

KAR 1

Johann Sebastian Bach: The Art of Fugue (81')

Bach: Canon alla decima

Arnold Dolmetsch 1907

2 CD Hungaroton HCD 32784-85, recorded 2015, (P) 2016

MACARIO SANTIAGO KASTNER

KAS 1

Soto: Tiento; Cabezón: Duniensela, Pavana Italiana, Diniensela

J &P Schiedmayer (Stuttgart Collection 62436)[4]

[LP?, Label unknown], recorded 1946

KAS 2

Storia della Musica Italiana 2

Frescobaldi: Partite sopra l'aria di Fiorenza; Pasquini: Partite sopra la Folia d'Espagne

LP RCA Italiana 40001-7, 1963

KAS 3

Música Española para Teclas de los Siglos XVI y XVII

Cabezón: Para quien crié yo cabellos, Himno a 3, Salve Regina; Tiento del Primer Tono, Diferencias sobre Guárdame las vacas, Otras Diferencias sobre Guárdame las vacas, Pavana Italiana, Diferencias sobre la Gallarda Milanesa; Correa: Tiento del V Tono, Tiento del VI Tono

Walter Merzdorf, Jacob Verwolf

LP MEC 1007, 1972

MACARIO SANTIAGO KASTNER and CREMILDE ROSADO FERNANDES

KAS 4

*Blanco: Concertos No.1, No.2; Olivares: Verso de Octava Tono

Walter Merzdorf

LP MEC 1008, 1972

CLAIRE KEVILLE

KEV 1

Irish Music on the Clavichord (43')

Trad: Planxty Saint Nicholas; Baile Uí Laoi, Love's a Tormenting Pain, Lord Galway's Lamentation, Michael O'Connor, Laments for Charles MacCabe & Sir Ulick Burke, Cremonea and Donal O'Brien, Mr O'Connor, Lament for Terence MacDonough, March of the Tribes, Lament of Loss, Sailing into Galway

John Morley

CD Custys Music Shop CKCD003, (p) 2015

IGOR KIPNIS

KIP 1

J. S. Bach on the Harpsichord and Clavichord

J. S. Bach: Preludes in C BWV924, in C BWV939, in c BWV999, in D BWV925, in d BWV926, in d BWV940, in e BWV941, in F BWV927, in F BWV928; Stölzel: Minuet in g; J. S. Bach: Trio in g BWV929, Preludes in g BWV930, in a BWV942, Prelude and Fughetta in C BWV870a, Fantasia in a BWV922, Adagio in G BWV968

Rutkowski and Robinette 1963

LP Epic BC 1332, recorded 1965, (P) 1966

KIP 1a

LP Epic LC 1332 [m/KIP 1]

KIP 1b

LP Columbia M30231 [r/KIP 1]

KIP 1c

*J. S. Bach: Preludes in C BWV924, in C BWV939, in c BWV999, in D BWV925, in d BWV926, in d BWV940, in e BWV941, in F BWV927, in F BWV928; Stölzel: Minuet in g; J. S. Bach: Trio in g BWV929, Preludes in g BWV930, in a BWV942

LP Columbia CBS 61214 [r/KIP 1]

KIP 1d (66')

*J. S. Bach: Preludes in C BWV924, in C BWV939, in c BWV999, in D BWV925, in d BWV926, in d BWV940, in e

BWV941, in F BWV927, in F BWV928; Stölzel: Minuet in g; J. S. Bach: Trio in g BWV929, Preludes in g BWV930, in a BWV942, Prelude and Fughetta in C BWV870a, Fantasia in a BWV922, Adagio in G BWV968

CD Sony Classical *Essential Classics* SBK 53 263 [r/KIP 1]

KIP 1e

C Sony Classical *Essential Classics* SBT 53 263 [f/KIP 1d]

KIP 2

German Music for Harpsichord and Clavichord (57')

C. P. E. Bach: Fantasia in C H291; Pachelbel: Partita on 'Werde munter Mein Gemüte'; Kuhnau: Biblical Sonata No.1, 'The Fight between David and Goliath'

Rutkowski and Robinette 1963

LP Epic BC 1363, 1967

KIP 2a

LP Epic LC 1363 [M/KIP 2]

KIP 2b

Europäische Cembalomusik des Barock und Rokoko

Pachelbel: Partita on 'Werde munte Mein Gemüte'

LP Columbia CBS S 77501 [r/KIP 2]

KIP 3

Austrian Music for Harpsichord and Clavichord (59')

Froberger: Suite No.26 in b; Mozart: Minuet in G K1e, Trio in

C K1f, Minuet in F K2, Allegro in Bb K3, Minuets in F K4, in F K5; Haydn: Sonata in G Hob.XVI:6

Rutkowski and Robinette 1963

LP Columbia Odyssey Y 30289, (P) [1971]

KIP 3a

100 Mozart Melodies (373')

Mozart: Minuet in G K1e, Trio in C K1f

5 CD Sony Classical SB5K 46 240 [r/KIP 3]

KIP 3b

100 Mozart Melodies Volume 2 (76')

CD Sony Classical SBK 46 242 [r/KIP 3a]

KIP 4

The Art of Igor Kipnis Vol.II

3 LP Columbia M3X 32325 (s/KIP 2, KIP 3]

KIP 5

*Scarlatti: Sonatas in b K87, in A K322-323

Rutkowski and Robinette 1963

LP Angel SZ-37310, recorded 1979

EM ix (1981) p.276

KIP 5a

Scarlatti Sonatas (67')

CD EMI Angel CDM-7 691182 [1987 r/KIP 5]

Gram (Jul 1988) p.215

KIP 5b

CD Musical Heritage Society MHS 513363W [r/KIP 5a]

KIP 5c

C Musical Heritage Society MHS 313363Z [f/KIP 5b]

KIP 6

*Anna Magdalena Bach Notebook (103')

J. S. Bach: Wen nur den lieben Gott BWV691, Aria in G BWV988i (from the Goldberg Variations), Prelude in C BWV846 (from *Das Wohltemperirte Clavier* Book 1); Petzold: Minuets in G and g BWVAnh 114-5; Stölzel: Bist du bei mir BWV508;[a] Böhm: Minuet in G; attrib Hasse: Polonaise in G BWVAnh 130; attrib C. P. E. Bach: March in D BWVAnh 122; attrib J. S. Bach: Minuet in G BWVAnh 116, Polonaise in F BWVAnh 117b, Minuet in Bb BWVAnh 118, Polonaise in g BWVAnh 119; J. S. Bach: Gib dich zufrieden BWV510, attrib J. S. Bach: Minuets in a BWVAnh 120, in c BWVAnh 121, Musette in D BWVAnh 126, Minuets in d BWVAnh 132, in F BWVAnh 113, Polonaise in F BWVAnh 117a, b (from Anna Magdalena Bach Book) [[a]with Judith Blegen, soprano]

2 LP Nonesuch DB79020, 1981

Gram (Feb 1982) p.1164

KIP 6a

2 CD Nonesuch 262802 [f/KIP 6]

KIP 6b

    2 CD Nonesuch 79020-2 [USA/KIP 6]

KIP 6c

    2 C Nonesuch D2-79020 [f/KIP 6b]

KIP 7

    Complete Fantasias by Bach (66')

    J. S. Bach: Fantasia in c BWV919, Fughetta in c BWV961, Fantasia in a BWV922, Chromatic Fantasia in d BWV903a

    Carl Fudge 1986 after Johann Christoph Georg Schiedmayer 1796

    CD Arabesque Z6577, recorded 1986, (P) 1987

    Gram (Jan 1988) p.1102, *OY* xix (1988) p.148

KIP 7a

    C Arabesque ABQC 6577 [f/KIP 7]

RALPH KIRKPATRICK

KIR 1

    J. S. Bach: 15 Two-part Inventions BWV772-786

    78 set Concert Hall Society C6, 1949

KIR 1a

    LP Concert Hall Society CHS 1088 [r/KIR 1]

KIR 1b

> Nixa CLYP 1088 [1953 r/KIR 1]
>
> *Gram* (Mar 1953) p.259, *RG* (1955) p.51

KIR 2

> J. S. Bach: *Das Wohltemperierte Klavier* Book 1 BWV846-869
>
> Arnold Dolmetsch 1932
>
> 2 LP Deutsche Grammophon Archiv SAPM 198311-2 , recorded 1959, (P) 1963
>
> *Gram* (Dec 1963) p.280

KIR 2a

> 2 LP Deutsche Grammophon Archiv APM 14311-2 [m/KIR 2]

KIR 2b

> 2 LP Deutsche Grammophon Archiv ARC 73211/2 [m USA/KIR 2]

KIR 2c

> 2 LP Deutsche Grammophon Archiv ARC 3211/2 [USA/KIR 2]

KIR 2d

> 2 LP Deutsche Grammophon 2708 006 [r/KIR 2]

KIR 2e

> **Ein armes tier ist das klavier*
>
> J. S. Bach: Prelude and Fugue in C BWV846
>
> CD Deutsche Grammophon 434 414-2 [r/KIR 2]

KIR 2f

    C Deutsche Grammophon 434 414-4 [f/KIR 2]

KIR 2g

    2 CD Deutsche Grammophon *The Originals* 463 601-2 [r/KIR 2]

    IRR (Aug 2000) p.75, *CCD* (Aug 2000) p.68, *PGCDY 2000/1* p.22, *CI* iv/2 (Nov 2000) p.56, *EMR* lxvii (Feb 2001), p.22, *ICD* p.11, *EM* xxix/4 (Nov 2001) p.659

KIR 2h

    16 CD Deutsche Grammophon *The Originals* 463 621-2 [s/KIR 2]

KIR 2i

    *Kleine chronik der Anna Magdalena Bach

    J. S. Bach: Prelude and Fugue in C BWV846 (excerpt)

    4 CD Deutsche Grammophon 463 913-2 [r/KIR 2]

KIR 2j

    4 C Deutsche Grammophon 463 913-4 [f/KIR 2i]

KIR 2k

    *J. S. Bach: The New Complete Edition (16880')

    J. S. Bach: Prelude and Fugue in F# BWV858

    222 CD + DVD Deutsche Grammophon 479 8000, (P) 2018 [see also DAR 3d, KIR 3c, KIR 5c, KIR 6d]

KIR 3

> J. S. Bach: *Das Wohltemperierte Klavier* Book 2 BWV870-893
>
> John Challis 1942
>
> 3 LP Deutsche Grammophon Archiv SLPM 139146-8, recorded 1967, (P) 1969

KIR 3a

> 2 CD Deutsche Grammophon *The Originals* 463 623-2 [r/KIR 3]
>
> *BBCMM* (Jul 2001) p.102, *EMR* 72 (July 2001) p.24, *EM* xxix/4 (Nov 2001) p.659, *CI* v/2 (Nov 2001) p.56

KIR 3b

> 15 CD Deutsche Grammophon *The Originals* 463 622-2 [s/KIR 3]

KIR 3c

> **J. S. Bach: The New Complete Edition* (16880')
>
> J. S. Bach: Preludes and Fugues in C# BWV872, in Eb BWV876, in f BWV881
>
> 222 CD + DVD Deutsche Grammophon 479 8000, (P) 2018 [see also DAR 3d, KIR 2k, KIR 5c, KIR 6d]

KIR 4

> 5 LP Deutsche Grammophon Archiv SAPM 198311-2 [r/KIR 2,3][5]

KIR 4a

> J. S. Bach: Preludes and Fugues in C BWV846, in c BWV847, in C# BWV848, in D BWV850, in E BWV854, in g BWV861,

in Ab BWV862, in Bb BWV866, in bb BWV867 (from *Das Wohltemperierte Klavier* Book 1 BWV846-869), in F BWV881, in F# BWV882, in G BWV884, in A BWV888, in b BWV893 (from *Das Wohltemperierte Klavier* Book 2 BWV870-893)

5 LP Deutsche Grammophon *Musikfest* 413 419-1 [r/KIR 4]

KIR 5

J. S. Bach: 6 Short Preludes BWV933-938, 12 Short Preludes BWV924-930, 939-942, 999, Applicato in C BWV994, Suites in a BWV818a, in Eb BWV819, Minuets in G BWV841, in g BWV842, in G BWV843

Dolmetsch 1932

LP Deutsche Grammophon Archiv SAPM 198178, 1960

Gram (Oct 1962) p.200, *RR* (Nov 1962) p.59

KIR 5a

LP Deutsche Grammophon Archiv APM 14178 [m/KIR 5]

KIR 5b

10 LP Deutsche Grammophon Archiv *New Bach Edition* Vol. 9 413 114-1 [s/KIR 5]

KIR 5c

***J. S. Bach: The New Complete Edition* (16880')

J. S. Bach: Preludes in d BWV924, in d BWV926, in F BWV927, in F BWV928, in g BWV930, Applicato in C BWV994, Minuets in G BWV841, in g BWV842, in G BWV843

222 CD + DVD Deutsche Grammophon 479 8000, (P) 2018 [s/KIR 6, see also DAR 3d, KIR 2k, KIR 3c, KIR 6d]

KIR 6

J. S. Bach: Two and Three-part Inventions

J. S. Bach: 15 Two-part Inventions BWV772-786, 15 Three-part Sinfonias BWV787-801

Dolmetsch 1932

LP Deutsche Grammophon Archiv SAPM 198179, 1960

Gram (Oct 1962) p.392, *RR* (Feb 1963) p.38

KIR 6a

LP Deutsche Grammophon Archiv APM 14179

[m/KIR 6]

KIR 6b

LP Deutsche Grammophon Archiv ARC 3174

[USA/KIR 6]

KIR 6c

*J. S. Bach: 15 Two-part Inventions BWV772-786, Prelude and Fugue in C BWV846 (from *Das Wohltemperirte Clavier* Book 1)

2 LP Deutsche Grammophon Privilege 2726 016 [1974 r/KIR 2, KIR 6]

PSRG 1975 p.33

KIR 6d

**J. S. Bach: The New Complete Edition* (16880')

222 CD + DVD Deutsche Grammophon 479 8000, (P) 2018 [s/KIR 6, see also DAR 3d, KIR 2k, KIR 3c, KIR 5c]

KIR 7

Bach: Harpsichord Works Volume 1

J. S. Bach: Suites in a BWV818a, in Eb BWV819, 15 Two-part Inventions BWV772-786, 15 Three-part Sinfonias BWV787-801, 6 Short Preludes BWV933-938, Applicato in C BWV994

11 LP Deutsche Grammophon Archiv *Bach Edition* Vol. 1 2722 015 [s/KIR 6]

Gram (Oct 1962) p.200, *RR* (Nov 1962) p.59, *Gram* (Jun 1975)

KIR 7a

10 LP Deutsche Grammophon Archiv *New Bach Edition* Vol. 11 413 114-1 [r/KIR 7]

KIR 7b

*Bach: Keyboard Music

10 LP Deutsche Grammophon Archiv 2722 020 [r/KIR 7]

Gram (Jan 1976)

KIR 7c

*Bach: Keyboard Music

LP Deutsche Grammophon Archiv 2547 031 [r/KIR 7]

KIR 7d

*Bach: Keyboard Music

C Deutsche Grammophon Archiv 3347 031 [r/KIR 7]

JOHN KITCHEN

KIT 1

Instruments from the Russell Collection (76')

J. S. Bach: Prelude and Fugue in Eb (from *Das Wohltemperierte Klavier* Book 2 BWV870-893)

Johann Adolph Hass 1763 (1)

CD Delphian DCD 34001, recorded 2000, (P) 2001

BBCMM (August 2001) p.97, *Early Music Today* X/i (Feb/Mar 2002) p.14

KIT 2

Instruments from the Russell Collection, Volume 2 (77')

J. C. F. Bach: March, Menuet, Adagio, Andante, March (from *Musikalisches Nebenstunden*, 1787-88)

Christian Gottlob Hubert 1784 (4)

CD Delphian DCD 34039, recorded 2005, (P) 2005

KIT 3

Instruments from the Rodger Mirrey Collection (76')

Anon: Almande prynce;[a] Fusi pavana piana;[a] Froberger: Lamento sopra la dolora pedita della Real Msta. Di Ferdinando IV, Re di Romani;[b] J. S. Bach: Suite in f BWV823[b]

[a]Anon fretted c.1620, [b]Anon unfretted c.1740

CD Delphian DCD34057, recorded 2008-10, (P) 2010

CHRISTOPHER KITE

KITa 1

Guillaume Dufay: Complete Secular Music

Dufay: Helas, et quant vous veray?, Portugaler

Jean Maurer 1975

6 LP L'Oiseau-Lyre D237 D6, recorded 1980, (P) 1981

Gram (Dec 1981) p.918, *PSRG 1984* p.356

KITa 1a

LP L'Oiseau-Lyre DSLO 611 [r/KIT 1]

Gram (Oct 1983) p.516

KITa 1b

5 CD L'Oiseau-Lyre 452 557-2 [r/KIT 1]

HORST KLAMMER

KLA 1

German Clavichord Music (54')

Hässler: Fantasia in e Op.17; C. P. E. Bach: Sonatas in A H72, in b H73; J. S. Bach: Fantasia in c BWV906; Türk: Sonata No.5 in e; C. P. E. Bach: Fantasia in f# H300

Martin Sassman 1974 after Christian Gottlob Hubert 1774 [sic]

LP Marus 308117Z, (P) 1981

KLA 1b

LP Marus/EMI Electrola ASD LC 8077 (v/KLA 1)

BERNHARD KLAPPROTT

KLAa 1

Georg Anton Benda: Six Sonatas für das Clavier (78')

Benda: Six Sonatas No.1-6 (1757)

Joseph Gottfried Horn 1788

CD Aeolus AE-10104, recorded 2005, (P) 2012

BCSN (Oct 2012) p.29, *CI* (May 2017) p.27

JEAN KLEEB

KLE 1

Viola da Samba: DE rio a RIO (61')

Barroso: Isso aqui o que é; Powell: Samba em Prelúdio; Jobim: Outra vez, Samba de uma nota só, Este seu olhar, Wave, Eu sei que vou te amar; Kleeb: Sambinha, Canto a Iemanjá, Improvisation, Improvisation, Gamba em prelúdio para Fernando; Barbosa: Trem das onze; Romero: Van y Vienen las olas; Trad arr Kleeb: Passa en la calle (Paranauê); Marais: Chaconne; Anon: Meis ollos van perlo mare; En una fuente; Trad: Murucututu; Queiroga: Ah, se eu vou [with Nadine Balbeisi (soprano), Fernando Marin (viola da gamba)]

Burkhard Zander 1996, Walter Merzdorf

CD Quartz Music QTZ 2121, rec 2015, (P) 2017

SEBASTIAN KNEBEL

KNE 1

Willst du dein Herz mir schenken …

Anon South German, c.1780

CD Bachhaus Eisenach [no number], recorded 2004

ROBERT KÖBLER (and harpsichord, organ)

KOB 1

Ein Konzert im Bachhaus Eisenach
J. S. Bach: Menuett Trio in g BWV929
LP ETERNA 8 25 715, 1974

TOBIAS KOCH

KOC 1

*Daniel Gottlob Türk, Johann Friedrich Reichardt, Carl Loewe (84')

Türk: Sechzig Handstücke für ausgehende Klavierspieler, 1792 (excerpts); Reichardt: 17 Klavierstücke über eine Petrarchische Ode, 1782

Carl Gottlob Sauer 1807

2 CD Querstand VKJK 1420, recorded 2013, (P) 2014

MIKKO KORHONEN

KOR 1

Svenska Klavikord: Mikko Korhonen Spelar Improvisationsmusik (73')

Korhonen: Improvisations in historical style - Glosas,[a] La Folia,[a] Praeludium and Fuga,[a] Voluntary,[a] Toccata,[b] Praeludium,[b] Allegro,[b] Toccata and Fuga,[b] Ouverture,[c] Suite,[c] Fantasia,[d] Rondo[d] ᵃGeorg Woytzig 1688, ᵇAnon, early 18th century, ᶜPhilip Jacob Specken 1743, ᵈMathias Petter Kraft 1806

CD SVEA Fonogram SVCD 8, recorded live 1995, (P) 1997

BCSN ix (Oct 1997) p.17, *CI* i/2 (Nov 1997) p.54, *ICD* p.12

KOR 2

Improvisations played by Mikko Korhonen (73')

Korhonen: 18 Improvisations in historical style

Pehr Lindholm 1791

CD SMS Musikmuseet [no number], recorded live 2006, (P) 2006

KOR 3

Improvisations played by Mikko Korhonen (53')

Korhonen: 10 Improvisations in historical style

Lindholm & Soderström 1808

CD SMS Musikmuseet [no number], recorded live 2006, (P) 2006

KOR 4

Improvisations played by Mikko Korhonen (56')

Korhonen: 16 Improvisations in historical style

Lindholm & Soderström 1807

CD SMS Musikmuseet [no number], recorded live 2006, (P) 2006

BARBARA KRAUS

KRA 1

Buttstedt: Claviersonaten (50')

Buttstett: Ständchen, Spinnerlied, Alla Polacca, Allegro, Sonate in Bb

Walter Merzdorf & Söhne

CD Medien Kontor Hamburg 080111, recorded 2006/7, (P) 2008

BEATE KRUPPKE

KRU 1

Musik zur nacht (60')

Sweelinck: Variations on 'Unter der Linden grüne'; Zachow: Mein schönste Zier; J. C. Bach: Mein schönste Zier; J. S. Bach: Sonata in d BWV964; Haydn: Aria and 12 Variations in Eb, Mozart: Sonatina in C; Bartók: Drei Tänze

Benedict Claas 1986 after Johann Adolf Hass 1761 & 1763

CD [no label or number], recorded 1999

MABEL KWAN

KWA 1

Inventions

Danny Clay: Inventions

C Bandcamp PT+ 008, recorded 2016

LINA LALANDI

LAL 1

Lina Lalandi plays the clavichord (73')

J. S. Bach: Preludes in C BWV924, in C BWV939, in c BWV999, in D BWV925, in d BWV926, in d BWV940, in e BWV941, in F BWV927, in F BWV928; Trio in g BWV929, Preludes in g BWV930, in a BWV942, Suite in e BWV996; C. P. E. Bach: Rondo in A H276, Rondo in e H272, 'Abschied von meinem Silbermannischen Claviere'; Couperin: Les idées heureuses (from Ordre No.2 in d), La favourite (from Ordre No.3 in c), Les moissoneurs, La gazoüillement, Le moucheron (from Ordre No.6 in Bb), Les fauvetes plaintives (from Ordre No.14 in d), Soeur Monique (from Ordre No.18 in d), Les tricoteuses (from Ordre No.23 in F), Les guirlandes (from Ordre No.24 in A), Les ombres errantes (from Ordre No.25 in c), L'épineuse (from Ordre No.26 in f#)

Thomas Goff 1939

CD English Bach Festival EBF 002 [private recordings], (P) 2002

CI vii/2 (Nov 2003) p.57

CHRISTIAN LAMBOUR

LAM 1

Friedrich Schorlemmer liest Texte von Dietrich Bonhoeffer

Walter Merzdorf, 1969

CD Accademia [no number], recorded 2015, (P) 2015

DANIEL LAUMANS

LAU 1

Claviermanuscripte aus Ávila, vol.1

Gaspar Smit, Haydn

Neupert

CD Ekcentrik [no number], recorded 2008

ALASTAIR LAURENCE

LAUa 1

*Laurence Let Loose: Jazz Improvisations on Early Keyboard Instruments (45')

Lennon & McCartney: Norwegian Wood

Pehr Lindholm & Henric Johan Söderström 1806

CD [No label or catalogue number], recorded live 1997

BCSN ix (Oct 1997) p.17

IRMGARD LECHNER

LEC 1

Tasten der Stille: Irmgard Lechner spielt Clavichord

Cabezon: Duos in d, in d; Fuenllana: Duo in d; Cabezon: Fabordon in a; Narváez: Guardame las vacas; Froberger: Tombeau in c, Toccata in d; J. S. Bach: Prelude in C BWV846 (from *Das Wohltemperierte Klavier* Book 1), Prelude in F BWV880 (from *Das Wohltemperierte Klavier* Book 2), Chromatic Fantasia in d BWV903, C. P. E. Bach: Les Folies d'Espagne H263

Wittmayer

CD [no label or number], recorded 1997, (P) 1997

BRADLEY LEHMAN

LEH 1

The Domestic Clavichord (111')

Anon: Estampie, En avois, Holloyne pardye, Quando claro; Attaingnant: Basse danse No.7; J. S. Bach: Minuets in G and g, O Haupt voll Blut und Wunden; C. P. E. Bach: Polonaises in g, G and g; Banchieri: Sonata prima; Bartók: For Children II: Nos. 5, 12, 13, 24, 2, 3, 14, 6, 7, 18; Böhm: Wer nur den lieben Gott; Debussy: Le petit negre; Gaultier: Tombeau de Mlle Gaultier; Gibbons: Song No.13; Legrand/Evans: You must believe in spring; Lehmann: Frosted toaster pastry and fugue, Ein feste Burg; Milan: Fantasia (Ricercar) No.67 in F, Ricercar (Fantasia) No.3 in G; Mudarra: Fantasia No.10; Narvaez: Guardame las vacas, Mille regretz (Cancion del emperador), Neusidler: Wie mocht ich fröhlich werden; Newman: Pavan; Pachelbel: O Haupt voll Blut und Wunden, Wenn wir in hochsten Noten sein, Warum betrubst du dich, mein Herz; Pass: Sultry; Paumann: Elend, du hast umfangen mich, Mit ganczem Willen; Caccini arr Philips: Amarilli mia bella, Galliard; Sancta Maria: Fantasia; Scheidt: O Haupt voll Blut und Wunden; Schoenberg: Piano piece Op.19/2; Schwartz: A rainy night in Rio; Tallis: A point; Trad arr Lehman: Song of the birds (Cant del ocells), The foggy morn, The piper o'er the meadows straying, Sakura; Van Soldt: Alman de la nonette; Victoria arr Lehman: O vos omnes; Walther: Jesu meine Freude

Carl Fudge kit after Hubert, built by Brian Joyce 1984, recorded 1999

(unreleased, available digitally)

LEH 2

Hymnal Masterworks: Clavichord (56')

Horn arr Lehman: Gaudeamus pariter (Ave virgo virginum);

Anon arr Lehman: Kremser/Grosser Gott, wir loben dich; Trad arr Lehman: Sakura; Vulpius arr Lehman: Lobt Gott den herren; Pachelbel: Wenn wir in hochsten Noten sein, Warum betrubst du dich, mein Herz; Lehman: Healing hem, Storm; Van Soldt: Alman de la nonette; Anon arr Lehman: Gabriel's message; Gibbons arr Lehman: Song No.13; J. S. Bach: O Haupt voll Blut und Wunden; Pachelbel: O Haupt voll Blut und Wunden; Scheidt: O Haupt voll Blut und Wunden; Anon arr Lehman: Christ ist erstanden; Luther arr Lehman: Ein feste Burg; Feliciano arr Lehman: Wasdin pang ipaad; Anon arr Lehman: Wunderbarer König; Walther: Jesu meine Freude, Herr Jesu Christ, dich zu uns wend; Böhm: Wer nur den lieben Gott; Trad arr Lehman: Dona nobis pacem (from *Hymnal: A Worship Book*)

Carl Fudge kit after Hubert, built by Brian Joyce 1984, recorded 1999

(unreleased, available digitally)

LEH 3

On a Tangent

Mp3.com 70078

CI v/2 (Nov 2001) p.57, *BCSN* (June 2002) p.26

LEH 4

On a Co-Tangent

Mp3.com 70125

CI v/2 (Nov 2001) p.57, *BCSN* (June 2002) p.26

LEH 5

Hymn Vignettes & Variations

Carl Fudge kit after Hubert, built by Brian Joyce 1984, recorded 1999

Mp3.com 70177

LEH 6

Dances with Clavichord

Carl Fudge kit after Hubert, built by Brian Joyce 1984, recorded 1999

Mp3.com 82919

LEH 7

The Serene Clavichord

Carl Fudge kit after Hubert, built by Brian Joyce 1984, recorded 1999

Mp3.com 82906

GUSTAV LEONHARDT

LEO 1

[Ilustrated talk on 'Good Taste']

[BBC Broadcast 1970]

LEO 2

*C. P. E. Bach: Sonatas, Rondos, Fantasies (86')

C. P. E. Bach: Fantasia in Bb H289, Sonata in D H286, Rondo in e H272, 'Abschied von meinem Silbermannischen Claviere', Fantasia in f# H300

Martin Skowroneck 1967 after Hass

2 LP Seon, recorded 1972, (P) 1972

LEO 2a

C. P. E. Bach: Sonatas, Rondos, Fantasies (86')

2 LP Pro Arte Seon 2PAL-2016 [1981 r/LEO 2]

LEO 2b

2 LP Pro Arte 248-2 [r/LEO 2]

LEO 2c

*(69')

C. P. E. Bach: Rondo in e H272, 'Abschied von meinem Silbermannischen Claviere', Fantasia in f# H300

CD RCA Victor GD 71969 [r/LEO 2]

LEO 2d

C. P. E. Bach: Sonatas, Rondos, Fantasies (86')

2 CD Sony SBK 61799 [r/LEO 2]

LEO 2e

Gustav Leonhardt Speelt op clavecimbel, hamerklavier, clavichord en orgel

C. P. E. Bach: Rondo in E Wq.66 [sic]

LP Philips 6833 187 [r/LEO 2]

LEO 3

Clavichord recital (68')

Ritter: Suite in f#; J. S. Bach: Fantasia and Fugue in a BWV904, French Suite No.2 in c BWV813; W. F. Bach: Polonaises No.6 in eb F12/6, No.8 in e F12/8, No.10 in F F12/10; C. P. E. Bach: Sonata in d H128, Sonatas in g H62, in b H73

Martin Skowroneck 1967

CD Philips 422 349-2, recorded 1988, (P) 1990

Gram (Aug 1990) p.392, *PGCD 1990* p.1272, *PGCDC 1992* p.1275

LEO 4

Böhm: Works for Keyboard (63')

Böhm: Suites No.1 in c, No.6 in Eb

Martin Skowroneck 1967

CD Sony Classical *Vivarte* SK 53114, recorded 1992

Gram (Sep 1993). p.85, *CCD* (Jul 1993) p.73, *PGCD 1996* p.188, *PGCD 1999* p.239

LEO 4a

Gustav Leonhardt Jubilee Edition - 80th Anniversary

15 CD DHM/Sony 8493525, (P) 2008

CARMEN LEONI

LEOa 1

Carlo Gesualdo da Venosa (1566–1613): Madrigals Book 2

Gesualdo: Canzon Francese

Copy of Anon, 17th century

CD Naxos 8.570549, rec 2007, (P) 2010

HAROLD LESTER

LES 1

*The Instruments of the Middle Ages and Renaissance

Anon: Le forze d'Hercole

2LP Vanguard VSD 71219/20

LES 1a

2 CD Vanguard Classics 8093 [1995 r/LES 1]

ROBERT LEVIN

LEV 1 [see HIL 1, PAY 1, VID 1]

*J. S. Bach 2000: The Millennium Edition

170 CD Hänssler, (P) 2000

LEV 2

*Hänssler Bach Edition Volume 116: The Well-Tempered Clavier, Book I (107')

J. S. Bach: Preludes and Fugues in C# BWV848, in d BWV852, in eb BWV853, in F BWV856, in F# BWV858, in Ab BWV862 (from *The Well-Tempered Clavier* Book I)

Rainer Schütze

2 CD Hänssler 92.116, recorded 2000, (P) 2000

EMR lxiv (Oct 2000) p.22, *Gram* (Nov 2000) p.87

LEV 3

*Hänssler Bach Edition Volume 117: The Well-Tempered Clavier, Book

II (136')

J. S. Bach: Preludes and Fugues in C# BWV872, in F BWV880, in f# BWV883, in A BWV888 (from *The Well-Tempered Clavier* Book II)

Jean Tournay 1991

2 CD Hänssler 92.117, recorded 2000, (P) 2000

EMR lxv (Nov 2000) p.20, *Gram* (Jan 2001) p.78

LEV 4

Bach: Werke für Tasteninstrumente

J. S. Bach: Preludes and Fugues in C# BWV848, in d BWV852, in eb BWV853, in F BWV856, in F# BWV858, in Ab BWV862 (from *The Well-Tempered Clavier* Book I),[a] Preludes and Fugues in C# BWV872, in F BWV880, in f# BWV883, in A BWV888 (from *The Well-Tempered Clavier* Book II)[b]

[a]Rainer Schütze, [b]Jean Tournay 1991

4 CD Master Music MM4204-2, (P) 2004 [s/LEV 2,3]

ROBERTO LOREGGIAN

LOR 1

Frescobaldi: Fioretti del Sig. Frescobaldi

CD Tactus TC 580603, (P) 1999

HANS LÜDEMANN

LUD 1

FutuRISM

Lüdemann: Futurism 5 "Das wahre Clavier"

[Wittmayer]

2 CD, JazzHausMusik JHM 92/93, recorded live 1997, (P) 1998

LUD 2

African Variations

Jobartheh/Lüdemann: Kora Suite

Wittmayer

CD RISM Edition 3001, recorded 2003, (P) 2003

LUD 3

Touching Africa [Trio Ivoire with Hans Lüdemann]

CD RISM Edition 3002, recorded 2005, (P) 2006

LUD 4

Kano [with Tata Dindin (kora, voice)]

Wittmayer

CD NRW 2032, recorded 2003, (P) 2005

ANDRUS MADSEN

MAD 1

Johann Pachelbel (155')

Madsen: Prelude [improvised]; Pachelbel: Suite in g PWC443, Christus der ist mein Leben PWC376, Suite in g PWC442

Christopher Clarke 1974 after South German instruments c.1700

2 CDs Raven OAR-919, recorded 2008, (P) 2010

BCSN (Feb 2011) p.23

BERNT MALMROS

MAL 1

Vårt kön så föga det behöfver - En musisk samvaro hemma hos Charlotte Cederström i februari 1808

[with Ann Hallenberg, mezzo]

Lindholm & Söderström 1808

CD Stockholms läns museum ABLMCD3, recorded 2002, (P) 2004

EDUARD MARTÍNEZ

MAR 1

*Antonio de Cabezón: Glosados, Diferencias, Tientos (60')

Antonio de Cabezón: Tiento XI Cum Sancto; Josquin arr
Antonio de Cabezón: Benedictus (Missa L'homme armé); Juan de Cabezón: Pues a mi desconsolado; Antonio Cabezón: Diferencias sobre la pavana Italiana

CD La mà de guido 2014, recorded 1995

JOVANKA MARVILLE

MARa 1

J. S. Bach: Keyboard Works (57')

J. S. Bach: Sonata in d BWV964, Preludes BWV939-943,

999, Vivaldi arr Bach, Concerto in D BWV972, Toccata in e BWV914, Partita in E BWV1006

Thomas Steiner 1999 after Christian Gottlob Hubert 1772

CD Passacaille 970, recorded 2011, (P) 2011

BCSN (Oct 2012) p.25

MATTHEW MCCONNELL

MCC 1

Canons on Clavichord (16')

Seitz: Celestine, Sphene, Tungsten, Amber, Spinel, Carnelian, Garnet, Ruby, Coral

CD/mp3/flac Bandcamp (2018)

ANNA MARIA McELWAIN

MCE 1

Hours well spent (79')

A. Gabrieli: Ricercar del primo tuono alla quarta alta; Byrd: A Galliards Gygge; J. S. Bach: Chromatic Fantasia and Fugue in d BWV903a; Beethoven: Sonata No.8 in c Op.13, 'Pathetique'; Lithander: Thema af Haydn, med variationer; Chopin: Preludes Op.28/3, 4, 14 and 15; Saint-Saëns: Suite pour piano, Op.90; Webern: Variations, Op.27/1; Ligeti: Capriccio No.2

Pehr Lindholm and Henric Johan Söderström 1808

CD Soundspheres RHLB10, recorded 2013, (P) 2013

CI (Nov 2014) p.23, *HFP* (Autumn 2014) p.35, *BCSN* (Feb 2015) p.25

MCE 2

Fux - Johnsen - Lithander - Beethoven (61')

Fux: Suite in g K404; Johnsen: Sonata No.6 in C; Lithander: Capriccio in G; Beethoven: Sonata No.3 in C Op.2/3

Stig Lundmark 2010

CD Soundspheres RHLB14, recorded 2014, (P) 2015

BCSN 63 (Oct 2015) p.13

NICHOLAS McGEGAN

MCG 1

Clavierbüchlein für Anna Magdalena Bach (74')

J. S. Bach: Prelude in C BWV846 (from *Das Wohltemperierte Klavier* Book 1); attrib C. P. E. Bach: Polonaise in F BWVAnh 117, Menuet in d BWVAnh 128; attrib Hasse: Menuet in G BWVAnh 130; attrib C. P. E. Bach: Polonaise in g BWVAnh 119 (from Anna Magdalena Bach Book)

Gary Blaise after Christian Gottlob Hubert 1789

CD Harmonia Mundi HMU 907042, recorded 1990, (P) 1991

Gram (Sep 1992) p.102

MCG 1a

C Harmonia Mundi HMU 407042 [f/MCG 1]

MCG 1b

CD Harmonia Mundi *Classical Express* HCX 3957042 [r/MCG 1]

PETER MEDHURST

[see RUTH DYSON]

JOHN METZ

MET 1

*May I have this Dance?

J. S. Bach: Partita No.1 in Bb BWV825

Allan Winkler

CD MetzMusic [no number], live recording

BARBARA MIEDEMA

MIE 1

The Seraphim Guide to Renaissance Music

Legrant: Wilhelmus Legrant (Buxheim Organ book); Facoli: Aria della Signora Moretta, Aria della Mareta Saporita

LP Seraphim LC 6052 and SIC-6052, 1970

TOMOKO AKATSU MIYAMOTO

MIY 1

The World of the Clavichord, Discovering a "Concealed" Realm (50')

Haydn: Sonatas in G Hob.XVI:6, in C Hob.XVI:48; C. P. E. Bach: 'Abschied von meinem Silbermannischen Claviere', Wq.66; Sonata in C Wq.62/10

Pehr Lindholm 1788

CD Hamamatsu Museum of Musical Instruments LMCD-1902,

recorded 2009, (P) 2010

BCSN (Oct 2010)

STEFANO MOLARDI

MOL 1

*Platti, Complete Music for Harsichord and Organ (236')

Platti: Sonata in g Op.4/4

Florindo Gazzola

3 CD Brilliant Classics 95518, recorded 2017, (P) 2018

FRANCIS MONKMAN

MON 1

Bach on Clavichord - I (79')

J. S. Bach: Preludes and Fugues in C BWV846, in E BWV854 (from *Das Wohltemperierte Klavier* Book 1), Preludes and Fugues in c BWV871, in G BWV884, in g# BWV887, in A BWV888, in B BWV892 (from *Das Wohltemperierte Klavier* Book 2), Partita No.6 in e BWV830

Hugh Gough 1958

CD [no number], recorded 2002

MON 2

Bach on Clavichord - II (33')

J. S. Bach: Duet No.1 in e BWV802, 15 Two-part Inventions BWV772-786, Sinfonias in C BWV787, in g BWV797 (from 15 Three-part Sinfonias BWV787-801)

Hugh Gough 1958

CD [no number], recorded 2002

GUIDO MORINI

MOR 1

Rolf Lislevand: Nuove Musiche (52')

Lislevand: Passacaglia cromatica, Passacaglia spontanea; Kapsberger arr Lislevand: Toccata [with ensemble, director Rolf Lislevand]

CD ECM New Series 1922 (476 3049), recorded 2004, (P) 2006

DAVITT MORONEY

MORa 1

William Byrd: The Complete Keyboard Music (497')

Byrd: Miserere I, Miserere II, Praeludium to the Fancy

Thomas Goff 1972

7 CD Hyperion CDA 66551/7, recorded 1991-2, 1996-7, (P) 1999

Gram (Oct 1999), p.77, *BBCMM* (Jan 2000), p.81, *EM* xxviii/3 (Aug 2000), p.494, *PGCDY 2000/1* p.91

MORa 1a

William Byrd: Keyboard Music

Byrd: Miserere I, Miserere II

CD Hyperion CDA 66558 [r/MORa 1]

MORa 2

    The Art of Fugue (24')

    J. S. Bach: Fughetta in C BWV952

    CD [CD accompanying Joseph Kerman, *The Art of Fugue: Bach Fugues for Keyboard, 1715-1750* (University of California Press, 2005)], (P) 2005

GAYLE MOSAND

MOS 1

    Klaver-Instrumenter på Ringve Museum (72')

    Berlin: Menuet in a

    Johann Christoph Fleischer 1728

    CD Ringve Museum RMCD 60.001, recorded 1979, (P) 1991

STEFAN MŰLLER

[see also JOHANN SONNLEITNER]

MUL 1

    J. S. Bach und Söhne: Empfindsame Claviermusik

    J. S. Bach: Choral partita on Sei gegrüsset, Jesu gütig BWV768; Rondo in e Wq.66, 'Abschied von meinem Silbermannischen Claviere', Rondo in C, 'Freude über den Empfang', Fantasia in f# H300, 'C. P. E. Bachs Empfindungen'

    Scheer & Vogel [2001] after attrib Johann Heinrich Silbermann c.1775

    CD Galerie Stilbruch, rec 2004

MUL 2

    BACH - ganz leise

    Reger: Drei zweistimmige Inventionen mit einer dritten Stimme versehen, in B, E and A [with Martin Pirktl, guitar]

    Scheer & Vogel [1996] after Jose Grabalos 1790

    CD Contrapunctus, recorded 2015, (P) 2016

PAMELA NASH

NAS 1

    Gary Carpenter: Die Flimmerkiste, Works for Ensemble (70')

    Carpenter: Van Assendelft's Vermeer

    Peter Bavington 1999

    CD NMC Records D111, recorded 2006, (P) 2007

    BCSN xli (Jun 2008) p.28

FRITZ NEUMEYER

NEU 1

    C. P. E. Bach: Sonata in A H270, Rondo in a H262

    Attrib Carl Christian Schmahl c.1805-1815

    [?LP] Deutsche Grammophon Archiv mono EPA 37120, 1950

    Gram (Jul 1960) p.73

NEU 1a

    [?LP] Parlophone PV.3403 [USA/NEU 1]

NEU 2

    J. S. Bach: Capriccio sopra la lontananza del suo fratro dilettissimo BWV992, 6 Short Preludes BWV933-938

    Martin Scholz after Georg Martin Gessinger 1780

    [?LP] Deutsche Grammophon Archiv AP 13038, 1955

    Gram (Jan 1957) p.299

NEU 2a

    J. S. Bach: Capriccio sopra la lontananza del suo fratro dilettissimo BWV992

    45rpm ep Deutsche Grammophon Archiv EPA 37015 [r/NEU 2]

NEU 3

    W. F. Bach: Sonata in A F8

    Attrib Carl Christian Schmahl c.1805-1815

    12" 78rpm Deutsche Grammophon Archiv EPA 37136, recorded 1951, (P) 1959

NEU 4

    Musik für Clavichord

    C. P. E. Bach: Rondo in C H260, Sonata in G H246, Fantasia in C H284; attrib Haydn: Sonatas in Bb Hob.XVI:2, in D Hob.XVI:14

    Attrib Carl Christian Schmahl c.1805-1815

    LP Deutsche Harmonia Mundi 1CO 65-99798

    EHM ii/6 (Apr 1980) p.154

NEU 4a

> *Research Period XX: Mannheim and Vienna*
>
> Attrib Haydn: Sonata in Bb Hob.XVI:2
>
> 7" EP Archiv Production EPA 37148 [v/NEU 4]

NEU 5

> *Claviermusik um 1780*
>
> C. P. E. Bach: Rondo in a H262,[a] Sonata in A H270;[a] Mozart: Sonata in C K545[b]
>
> [a]Attrib Carl Christian Schmahl c.1805-1815, [b]Anon South German 18th century
>
> LP Toccata FSM 43604 [?r/NEU 4]

NEU 5a

> *Original Instruments, Vol.3*
>
> 3 LP Telefunken 6.35576, (P) 1981 [r/NEU 5]

NEU 6

> *Haydn Sonatas Vol.1*
>
> Haydn: Sonata in D Hob.XVI:4; attrib Haydn: Sonatas in G Hob.XVI:8, in C Hob.XVI:10, in G Hob.XVI:11; Haydn: Sonata in A Hob.XVI:12; attrib Haydn: Sonatas in D Hob.XVI:14, in Eb Hob.XVI:16, in Bb [Henle No.2]
>
> Attrib Carl Christian Schmahl c.1805-1815
>
> 3 LP 3-Vox SVBX-573, 1962

NEU 6a

> 3 LP Vox VBX-73 [m/NEU 6]

NEU 7

    Plaudereien über Fritz Neumeyer: Hannsdieter Wohlfarth erinnert sich

    2 CD [no label], (P) 2006

ANTHONY NEWMAN

NEW 1

    *J. S. Bach: Preludes in C# BWV848, in E BWV854, in F BWV856, in f# BWV859, in B BWV868 (from *Das Wohltemperierte Klavier* Book 1)

    2 LP CBS Columbia M2 32875

NEW 1a

    Complete Collected Harpsichord Works of J S Bach

    J. S. Bach, Prelude in B major (Well-Tempered Clavier, Book 2)

    10 CD 903 Records 8550

LINDA NICHOLSON

NIC 1

    Tage Alter Musik in Herne 1989: Vom Versuch zur Schöpfung Musik in Deutschland zwischen 1750 und 1800 (224')

    C. P. E. Bach: Variations on 'Les Folies d'Espagne' H263, Sonata in a Wq.50

    Johann Adolph Hass 1767

    3 CD WDR [West German Radio] D-7378/80, recorded live 1989, (P) 1989

NIC 2

    Edition Carl Philipp Emanuel Bach 7: Sonatas, Clavierstücke (63')

    C. P. E. Bach: Sonatas in a H138, in G H137, in d H139, *Kurze Und Leichte Clavierstücke* H193-203, H228-238

    Johann Adolph Hass 1767

    CD Capriccio 10 318, recorded 1988, (P) 1991

    BCSN 52 (Feb 2012) p.18

HIROAKI OOI

OOI 1

    J. S. Bach: Die Kunst der Fuge

    J. S. Bach: The Art of Fugue BWV1080

    Joris Potvlieghe 2008 after Saxon models

    CD ENZO Recordings EZCD-10004, rec 2008, (P) 2009

NAOYA OTSUKA

OTS 1

    *Clavis: Baroque organ, harpsichord and clavichord music

    Johann Kreiger: Menuet in a; Fischer: Chaconne in a; Bach: Prelude in G, BWV1007, Prelude in C BWV846

    CD ALM Records ALCD-1115, (P) 2010

ANNA PARADISO

PAR 1

    *J. H. Roman: The 12 Keyboard Sonatas, Nos.1-7 (72')

Roman: Sonatas No.6 in Bb, No.7 in F

Dan Johansson 1997 after Philip Jakob Specken 1743

CD BIS BIS-2095, recorded 2013 (P) 2014

EMR (Feb 2015) p.23

PAR 2

*J. H. Roman: The 12 Keyboard Sonatas, Nos.8-12 (77')

Roman: Sonatas No.10 in b, No.11 in f

Dan Johansson 1997 after Philip Jakob Specken 1743

CD BIS BIS-2135, recorded 2014, (P) 2015

BCSN (Oct 2009) p.21

PAR 3

*Anna Paradiso plays Paradisi on harpsichord, clavichord & fortepiano (88')

Pietro Domenico Paradisi: Sonatas No.2 in Bb, No.4 in g, No.5 in F (1754)

Pehr Lindholm 1792

CD BIS BIS-2415, recorded 2018, (P) 2020

JOSEPH PAYNE

PAY 1 [see also HIL 1, LEV 1, VID 1]

*J. S. Bach 2000: The Millennium Edition

170 CD Hänssler, (P) 2000

PAY 2

*Hänssler Bach Edition Volume 137: Klavierbüchlein für Wilhelm Friedemann Bach (123')

J. S. Bach: Allemandes BWV836-7, Bass-skizze in g BWV953, Menuets BWV841-3, Preludes BWV772-86, BWV924, BWV847-8, BWV850, BWV853, BWV856

Johannes Mayer after attrib Gottfried Silbermann 1723

2 CD Hänssler 92.137, recorded 1999, (P) 1999

EMR lvi (Dec 1999) p.26, *Gram* (Dec 1999) p.85, *CCD* (May 2000) p.80, *PGCDY* 2000/1 p.20, *HFM* ix/2 (Summer 2001) p.34

PAY 2b

An Introduction to the Complete Works of Johann Sebastian Bach

J. S. Bach: Prelude in c BWV847a

CD Hänssler 92.920, (P) 1999

PAY 3

Bach: Werke für Tasteninstrumente

J. S. Bach: Allemandes BWV836-7, Bass-skizze in g BWV953, Menuets BWV841-3, Preludes BWV772-86, BWV924, BWV847-8, BWV850, BWV853, BWV856

Johannes Mayer after attrib Gottfried Silbermann 1723

4 CD Master Music MM4206-2, (P) 2004 [r/PAY 2]

PAY 4

Pachelbel: Complete Organ Works, Volume 11

Johann Mayer 1997 after J. J. Donat 1700

CD Centaur CRC2491, rec 1998, (P) 2001

GUY PENSON

PEN 1

*Mozart: Keyboard works (175')

Mozart: Andante in C K1a, Allegro in C K1b, Allegro in F K1c, Minuets in F K1d, G K1e, C K1f, Allegro in F K15a, Allegro in F K15m

3 CD Ricercar RIC05081, recorded 1991

Gram (Dec 1992)

PEN 1a

*Mozart Edition, volume 13: Keyboard Works (613')

10 CD Brilliant Classics 99723 [s/PEN 1]

PEN 1b [see also BEL 1]

**Mozart Complete Works*

170 CD Brilliant Classics 92540 [s/PEN 1]

JULIAN PERKINS

PER 1

Dialogues: The Music of Stephen Dodgson, Volume 2 (59')

Dodgson: Suite No.1, Suite No.2

Karin Richter 1998 after Christian Gottlob Hubert 1771

CD Campion Cameo 2088, recorded 2008, (P) 2009

BCSN (Oct 2009) p.21

PER 2

Bach French Suites (67')

J. S. Bach: French Suites Nos.1 in d BWV812,[a] No.2 in c BWV 813,[b] No.3 in b BWV814,[b] No.4 in Eb BWV815,[b] No.5 in G BWV816,[a] No.6 in E BWV817;[a] Froberger: Partita No.2 in d FbWV602;[a] Telemann: Suite in A TWV32:14[b]

[a]Peter Bavington 2005 after attrib Johann Heinrich Silbermann c.1775, [b]Peter Bavington 2008 after J. J. Bodechtel c.1785

2 CD Resonus RES10163, recorded 2015, (P) 2016

BCSN (Oct 2016) p.19, CI (Nov 2016) p.59

PER 3

Herbert Howells: Complete Clavichord Works (86')

Howells: Lambert's Clavichord Op.41;[a] Howells' Clavichord[b/c]

[a]Arnold Dolmetsch 1925, [b]Thomas Goff 1952 (Goff's Fireside, Patrick's Siciliano only), [c]Peter Bavington 2005 after attrib Johann Heinrich Silbermann c.1775

2 CD Prima Facie PFCD065/66, recorded 2016, (P) 2017

BCSN (Jun 2018) p.7

PER 4

Music for a King – Chamber works from the Court of Frederick the Great (99')

C. F. Fasch: Andantino con VII Variazioni in G Op.17

Karin Richter 1998

2 CD Channel Classics CCS 41819, rec 2018, (P) 2019

MATS PERSSON

PERa 1

Klavikord (59')

Elköf: Nodes No.1,[d] 2,[b] 3,[c] 4,[d] 5,[c] 6,[d] 7;[b] Persson: Khroma,[c] Rust;[cd] Elköf and Persson:[a] Blue Bell,[ac] Bole,[ab] Teal,[ad] Icterine[ad] [with Andreas Elköf (zither)[a]]

Pehr Lundborg 1778,[b] Lindholm & Söderstrom 1808,[c] Ragnar Köhlin 1996[d]

CD Compunctio CompCD008, recorded 2012, (P) 2013

OSCAR PETERSON

PET 1

Porgy and Bess

Gershwin: Summertime, Bess, you is my woman, My man's gone now, It ain't necessarily so, I loves you, Porgy, I got plenty O' nuttin', O Bess, oh where's my boat, They pass by singin', There's boat dat's leavin' soon for New York, Strawberry woman (from Porgy and Bess) [with Joe Pass (guitar)]

Morley 1976

LP Pablo 2310 779, recorded 1976, (P) 1976

PET 1a

C Pablo 2310779

PET 1b

CD Ace Pablo 2310779

PET 1c

    CD Verve 519807

PET 1d

    CD Ace *Original Jazz Classics* OJCCD 829

CESARE PICCO (and electronic piano[a])

PIC 1

Original Sin (40')

Picco: Aria 54,[b] Original Sin,[b] Stupor Mundi,[ab] Dance of Conspiracy,[b] Black Tower,[ab] Aria 108,[ab] Love Enigma[ab] [with Sezione Aurea (string quartet)[b]]

Roberto Marioni 2011 after attrib Johann Heinrich Silbermann c.1775

CD Edizioni Ishtar SSB035, (P) 2015

ANNELISE PFLUGBEIL

PFL 1

J. S. Bach: Gib dich zufrieden BWV511; attrib J. S. Bach: Minuet in c BWVAnh 121; attrib C. P. E. Bach: March in Eb BWVAnh 127; J. S. Bach: Aria in G BWV988i (from the Goldberg Variations); attrib J. S. Bach: Polonaise in g BWVAnh 119; Minuets in d BWVAnh 132, in G BWVAnh 116 (from Anna Magdalena Bach Book), Allemande in g BWV836, Menuet in g BWV842; J. S. Bach: Wen nur den lieben Gott BWV691 (from Wilhelm Friedmann Bach Book); Telemann: Suite in A BWV824

7" Cantate 643564, 1962

PFL 1a

    7" Cantate T72099F [m/PFL 1]

    Gram (Jan 1962) p.357

EDITH PICHT-AXENFELD

PIC 1

    J. S. Bach: *Das Wohltemperierte Klavier* Book 2 BWV870-893 (excerpts)

    BBC Sound Archives T34505 (July 1968)

LUITGARD PÖHLERT

POH 1

    Songs and settings from the Liederbuch of Arnt von Aich

    LP Musical Heritage Society IU 1914H

EVA MARIA POLLERUS

POL 1

    Carl Philipp Emanuel Bach: Sonatas for Flute & Basso Continuo (72')

    C. P. E. Bach: Flute Sonata in G H561 [with Katalin Horvath (flute)]

    Karin Richter 1998 after Christian Gottlob Hubert 1771

    CD TYXart TXA 15056, recorded 2013, (P) 2015

    BCSN (Jun 2016) p.18

GHISLAIN POTVLIEGHE

POT 1

Abraham van den Kerckhoven (1618-1701)

Ghislain Potvlieghe 1973

CD Dulce Melos A-2009, recorded 2009

SIEGBERT RAMPE

RAM 1

*Johann Jacob Froberger: The Unknown Works Vol. 1 (71')

Froberger: Partitas in g FBWV641, in c FBWV644, Sarabande in c FBWV640

Jörg Gobeli 2000 after Anon South German/Austrian c.1670

CD Dabringhaus & Grimm MDG 341 1186-2, recorded 2003, (P) 2003

RAM 2

*Johann Jacob Froberger: The Unknown Works Vol. 2

Froberger: Partita Mayrin, Partita in e FBWV648

Jörg Gobeli 2000 after Anon South German/Austrian c.1670

CD Dabringhaus & Grimm MDG 341 1195-2, recorded 2003, (P) 2004

RAM 3

*Muffat: Complete Clavier Works (61')

Muffat: Partita in C

Jörg Gobeli 2000 after anon South German instrument, c.1670

CD Dabringhaus & Grimm MDG 341 1213-2, recorded 2003, (P) 2004

RAM 4

Jan Pieterszoon Sweelinck: Keyboard Works (79')

Sweelinck: Paduana Lachrimae collorirt,[a] Mein junges Leben hat ein Endt[b]

[a]Jörg Gobeli 2000 after Anon South German/Austrian c.1670, [b]Martin Kather 1999 after Anon Italian c.1540

CD Dabringhaus & Grimm MDG 341 1256-2, recorded 2003, (P) 2003

RAM 5

Peter Philips: Keyboard Works, vol.1

Philips: Pavana Dolorosa cum Galiarda,[a] Galliard in a;[a] Striggio arr Philips: Chi fara fede al cielo;[a] Lassus arr Philips: Bonjour mon coeur[b]

[a]Jörg Gobeli 2000 after Anon South German/Austrian c.1670, [b]Martin Kather 1999 after Anon Italian c.1540

CD Dabringhaus & Grimm MDG 341 1257-2

RAM 6

John Bull: Walsingham – Organ and Keyboard Works (81')

Bull: The Duke of Brunswick's Alman,[a] Fantasia in d,[a] Dr Bull's Chromatic Pavan & Galliard,[a] Ut re mi fa sol la,[a] Dr Bull's My Self,[b] The Duchess of Brunswick's Toy[b]

[a]Jörg Gobeli 2000 after Anon South German c.1670, [b]Martin Kather 1999 after Anon Italian c.1540

CD Dabringhaus & Grimm MDG 341 1258-2, recorded 2004, (P) 2005

RAM 7

> *Mozart: Complete Clavier Works Vol. 1 (75')*
>
> Mozart: Thema in F K54, [Menuetto] in F K2, [Piece] in Bb K15ii, [Piece] in Bb KAnh 109b/9, [Menuetto] in Ab K109b/8, 8 Menuets K315a
>
> Dietrich Hein 2002 after Christian Ernst Friederici 1765
>
> CD Dabringhaus & Grimm MDG 341 1301-2, recorded 2004, (P) 2005

RAM 8

> *Mozart: Complete Clavier Works Vol. 2*
>
> Dietrich Hein 2002 after Christian Ernst Friederici 1765
>
> CD Dabringhaus & Grimm MDG 341 1302-2, recorded 2004, (P) 2005

RAM 9

> *Mozart: Complete Clavier Works Vol. 3 (77')*
>
> Mozart: Variations on a Minuet by Fischer K179
>
> Dietrich Hein 2002 after Christian Ernst Friederici 1765
>
> CD Dabringhaus & Grimm MDG 341 1303-2, recorded 2004, (P) 2006

RAM 10

> *Mozart: Complete Clavier Works Vol. 4 (80')*
>
> Mozart: [Clavierstück] K15mm, K15oo, K15pp, K15qq, K33B, K626B, K15h
>
> Martin Scholz 1970 after Johan David Schiedmayer 1791
>
> CD Dabringhaus & Grimm MDG 341 1304-2, recorded 2005, (P) 2006

RAM 11

Mozart: Complete Clavier Works Vol. 5 (77')

Mozart: Andante in C K1a, Allegro in C K1b, Allegro in C K1c, Menuetto in F K1d, [Menuetto] and Trio K1e-f, [Clavierstück] in C K9a

Martin Scholz 1970 after Johan David Schiedmayer 1791

CD Dabringhaus & Grimm MDG 341 1305-2, recorded 2005, (P) 2006

RAM 12

Mozart: Complete Clavier Works Vol. 6 (81')

Mozart: Allegro in Bb K3, Sonata No.4 in Eb K282

Martin Scholz 1970 after Johan David Schiedmayer 1791

CD Dabringhaus & Grimm MDG 341 1306-2, recorded 2005, (P) 2007

RAM 13

Mozart: Complete Clavier Works Vol. 7 (80')

Mozart: Variations in Bb K24, in G K25, [Clavierstück] in C K15s, Marche funbre in c K453a

Allan Winkler 2003 after Johann Christoph Georg Schiedmayer 1796

CD Dabringhaus & Grimm MDG 341 1307-2, recorded 2007, (P) 2007

RAM 14

Mozart: Complete Clavier Works Vol. 8 (79')

Mozart: [Menuet] in F K4, [Clavierstück] in F K15m,

[Clavierstück] in C K15n, [Menuet] in F K5, 12 Menuets K176, [Clavierstück] in F K15a, [Clavierstück] in C K15b, [Menuetto] in G K15c, [Clavierstück] in D K15d

Allan Winkler 2003 after Johann Christoph Georg Schiedmayer 1796

CD Dabringhaus & Grimm MDG 341 1308-2, recorded 2007, (P) 2008

RAM 15

Peter Philips: Complete Keyboard Works, vol.2 (73')

Philips: Galliarda; Marenzio arr Philips: Ecco l'aurora, Liquide perle amor; Tomkins arr Philips: Pavana Anglica, collerirt; Caccini arr Philips: Amarilli di Julio Romano

Jörg Gobeli 2000 after Anon South German/Austrian c.1670

CD Dabringhaus & Grimm MDG 341 1435-2, recorded 2004, (P) 2008

EMR 124 (April 2008) p.27

RAM 16

Mozart: Complete Clavier Works Vol.10

Martin Scholz 1970 after Johan David Schiedmayer 1791

CD Dabringhaus und Grimm MDG 341 1310-2, rec 2005/7, (P) 2009

RAM 17

Mozart: Complete Clavier Works Vol.11

Allan Winkler 2003 after Johann Christoph Georg Schiedmayer 1796

CD Dabringhaus und Grimm MDG 341 1311-2, rec 2007, (P) 2010

RAM 18

    Mozart: Complete Clavier Works Vol.12 (78')

    Mozart: [Clavierstück] in C K15f, [Clavierstück] in G K15e, [Clavierstück] in D K15c, [Clavierstück] in g K15r, [Menuetto] in G K15y

    Allan Winkler 2003 after Johann Christoph Georg Schiedmayer 1796

    CD Dabringhaus & Grimm MDG 341 1312-2, recorded 2007, (P) 2011

LAYTON RING

RIN 1

    A Concert of Early Music

    J. S. Bach: Prelude and Fugue in G BWV884 (*Das Wohltemperierte Klavier* Book 2); Couperin: Prélude No.1 in C (from *L'Art de Toucher le Clavecin*)

    [Dolmetsch]

    LP Chantry CRLP 2, [1960]

RIN 1a

    C Chantry [f/RIN 1]

RIN 2

    The Concert

    J. S. Bach: 5 Short Preludes BWV933-937, Preludes and Fugues in C BWV846, in D BWV850, in Bb BWV866 (from *Das Wohltemperierte Klavier* Book 1)

[Dolmetsch]

LP Chantry CRLP 12

RIN 2a

C Chantry [f/RIN 2]

RIN 3

Les Agréments

Froberger: Suite No.15 in a; Rameau: La Joyeuse, L'Entretien des Muses

[Dolmetsch]

LP Chantry CRLP 14

RIN 3a

C Chantry [f/RIN 3]

RIN 4

Courtly Masquing Ayres

J. S. Bach: Chromatic Fantasia and Fugue in d BWV903

[Dolmetsch]

LP Chantry CRLP 15

RIN 4a

C Chantry [f/RIN 4]

RIN 5

L'Amour de Moy

Scarlatti: Sonatas in F# K44, in A K208-209

[Dolmetsch]

LP Chantry CRLP 16

RIN 5a

C Chantry [f/RIN 5]

RIN 6

Les Festes Vénitiennes

J. S. Bach: Prelude and Fugue in F BWV881 (from *Das Wohltemperierte Klavier* Book 2)

[Dolmetsch]

LP Chantry CRLP 17

RIN 6a

C Chantry [f/RIN 6]

RIN 7

The Music Room

J. S. Bach: Prelude and Fugue in d BWV851 (from *Das Wohltemperierte Klavier* Book 1)

[Dolmetsch]

LP Chantry CRLP 18

RIN 7a

C Chantry [f/RIN 7]

RIN 8

> *A Garland of Music*
>
> Pergolesi: Variations; Lully: Bourrée et Menuet d'Achille (from Achille et Polyxene)
>
> [Dolmetsch]
>
> LP Chantry CRL(P) 19

RIN 8a

> C Chantry [f/RIN 8]

RIN 9

> *Apollo's Feast – The Dolmetsch Collection, instruments from the 15th to 19th centuries*
>
> [Dolmetsch]
>
> LP Abbey PHB 731, (P) 1973

TIM ROBERTS

ROB 1

> W. F. Bach: Polonaises No.9 in F F12/9, No.10 in F F12/10, No.5 in Eb F12/5; C. P. E. Bach: Rondo in G Wq.59/2, Fantasia in C Wq.[59]/6; J. C. F. Bach: Solfeggio in D
>
> [BBC Broadcast 1995]

JOHN ROBINSON

ROBa 1

> *Praeludium (58')

Buxtehude: Fugue in C; Byrd: Fantasias in a, in C; Philips: Pavane

John Morley

CD Syrinx S26404, recorded 2003

CHRISTOPH ROUSSET

[see CHRISTOPHER HOGWOOD]

GERGELY SÁRKÖZY

SAR 1

Music to Entertain the Kings of Hungary 1490-1526
Finck: Ich wird erlost; Hofhaimer: Carmen Magistri Pauli; Nach willen dein

2 LP Hungaroton SPLX 11983-84, (P) 1979

Gram (Feb 1981) p.1113

SAR 1a

2 LP Hungaroton GU 11983-84T [v/SAR 1]

JOSEPH SAXBY

SAX 1

*Byrd: Pavan Earl of Salisbury (excerpt)

BBC Sound Archives 15568 (July 1950)

SAX 2

The Dolmetsch Collection

J. S. Bach: Prelude in F BWV881 (from *Das Wohltemperierte Klavier* Book 2)

[Dolmetsch]

LP Dolmetsch

GUDRUN MARGARETHE SCHMEISER

SCH 1

The Triumph of Maximilian I

Hofhaimer: Carmen Magistri Pauli

LP Nonesuch HB-73016, recorded c.1965

MARTINA SCHOBERSBERGER

[see GUSTAV AUZINGER]

ARTHUR SCHOONDERWOERD

SCHa 1

"*Pastime with good company*" 1998 – 2003

Beethoven: Für Elise

Joris Potvlieghe

CD Alpha 901, recorded 2003

SCHa 2

*Mozart: Complete Clavier Sonatas (346')

Mozart: Sonatas in F K322, in Bb K333, in C K545, in D K576

Joris Potvlieghe 2005 after North German c.1780

6 CD Accent ACC 24254, recorded 2005, 2009, (P) 2013

CHRISTINE SCHORNSHEIM

SCHb 1

*Joseph Haydn: Die Klavier sonaten (886')

Haydn: Sonatas No.9 in D Hob.XVI:4, No.11 in Bb Hob.XVI:2, Arietta No.1 in Eb Hob.XVII:3, Sonatas No.12 in A Hob.XVI:12, No.14 in C Hob.XVI:3, No.29 in Eb Hob.XVI:45, Fragment in c Hob.XVI:20

Burkhard Zander 1999 after Joseph Gottfried Horn 1788

14 CD Capriccio 49 404, recorded 2003-4, (P) 2005

WINFRIED SCHRAMMEK

SCHc 1

*Historische Meisterinstrumente: Harpsichord, Hammerflügel, Clavichord

Kuhnau: Partita No.4 in f;[a] C. P. E. Bach: Sonata in b[b]

[a]Johann Jacob Donat 1700, [b]attrib G. Silbermann

LP Acanta 23-506, recorded 1976-77, (P) 1982

SCHc 1a

*Historische Meisterinstrumente (103')

2CD Membran 233567, (P) 1982

SCHc 1b

*Historische Meisterinstrumente (103')

2CD Acanta 233567 [v/SCHd 1a]

SCHc 2

Historische Tasteninstrumente aus dem Musikinstrumenten-Museum der Universität Leipzig (65')

Gardane: Passemezzo nuovo from Intabulatora ... per ... manachordi (1551)

Domenico Pisaurensis 1543

CD Querstand VKJK 9501 [r/THA 1f], recorded 1994, (P) 1995

WOLFGANG SCHRÖDER

SCHd 1

J. K. F. Fischer: Musicalischer Parnassus

Fischer: Musicalischer Parnassus

Cornelius Bom 1992 after Hieronymous Albrecht Hass 1742

2 CD Sirod Musikproduktion, recorded 2010

BCSN (Jun 2012) p.20, *CI* (May 2012) p.29

CLAUDIA SCHWEITZER

SCHe 1

*O süsser Ton

Haydn: Deutsche Lieder, Arianna a Naxos [with Susanne Lohmiller (mezzo)]

Jürgen Ammer 1997 after Johann Christoph Georg Schiedmayer 1787

2 CD Upala 99021

BEATA SEEMAN

SEE 1

Raume um Mozart

[with Klaus Holsten, flute]

Matthias Kramer [2003] after Tannenberg MS

CD Sona Records 1004, (P) 2008

LISELOTTE SELBIGER

SEL 1

J. S. Bach: Preludes BWV933-938, Four Duets Nos.3 and 4, BWV804-805; C. P. E. Bach Sonata No.5 in F major Wq.55

Hanns Neupert

LP, recorded 1952

SEL 1a

Liselotte Selbiger plays Purcell, Couperin, Bach, Scarlatti, Rameau (105')

2 CD Danacord DACOCD 645, (P) 2005 [r/SEL 1]

ELLA SEVSKIKH

SEV 1

*Baroque Keyboard (36')

J. S. Bach: Chromatic Fantasia in d BWV903

David Bolton

C Huntcliff Recording Services HRS 376

PAUL SIMMONDS

SIM 1

Mozart: Fantasia in d K385g; C. P. E. Bach: Sonata in A H270; Carvalho: Toccata in g

Pehr Lundborg 1775

C [Private recording], recorded live 1991

SIM 2

Deutsche Clavichord-Musik (80')

Buxtehude: Praeludium in g BuxWV163;[a] Kuhnau: Biblical Sonata No.4, 'Hezekiah, Sick unto Death and Restored to Health';[a] Müthel: Arioso and Variations in c; W. F. Bach: Sonata No.5 in D F4;[b] Türk: Sonata in a (1776 No.5);[a] Hässler: Sonata in d (1780 No.3)[b]

[a]Karin Richter 1986 after Johann Jacob Bodechtel c.1750, [b]Karin Richter after Christian Gottlob Hubert 1771

CD Ars Musici AM 1145-2, recorded 1994, (P) 1995

BCSN iv (Feb 1996) p.16, *EM* xxiv/4 (Nov 1996) p.716, *ICD* p.12

SIM 3

Ernst Wilhelm Wolf: Keyboard Sonatas (76')

Wolf: Sonata in c, in Bb (1779 No.2), in c (1775 No.3), in Bb (1774 No.1), in c (1785 No.1), in d (1774 No.3), in F, in e (1793 No.5), in Bb (1775 No.5), in b (1775 No.6)

Karin Richter 1986 after Christian Gottlob Hubert 1771

CD Ars Musici AM 1206-2, recorded 1997, (P) 1997

Tangents iii (Fall 1997), p.5, *BCSN* ix (Oct 1997) p.17, *CI* 1/2

(Nov 1997) p.54, *Gram* (Mar 1998) p.116, *EMR* (Jun 2001) p.21, *HFM* ix/2 (Summer 2001) p.38, *ICD* p.12

SIM 4

'Pour ung Plaisier': Renaissance Keyboard Music on the Clavichord (68')

Anon: J'ay pris amours, Fantasy in fa; La cara cossa del Berdolin, La Canella, La franzoxina; Son quel duca de Milano, La lodexana, Upon La Mi Re, Beata viscera, Felix namque; ap Rhys: Felix namque; Binchois: Adieu mes tres belle, Esclave puist yl; Brumel: Tandernack; Buchner: La spania in re; Crequillon arr A. Gabrieli: Pour ung Plasir; A. Gabrieli: Capriccio sopra Il Pass'e mezzo Antico; Hofhaimer: Ain frewlich wesenn; Merulo: Canzon a 4, dita 'La Bovia'; Philips: Pavana e Galiarda Dolorosa; Redford: Felix namque; Sweelinck: Fantasia chromatica

Karin Richter 1993 after Domenicus Pisaurensis 1543

CD Ars Musici AM 1378-2, recorded 2003, (P) 2004

CI viii/2 (Nov 2004) p.57

SIM 5

W. F. Bach: Polonaises & Fugues (80')

W. F. Bach: 12 Polonaises F12, 8 Fugues F31

Pehr Lindholm 1780

CD London Independent Records LIR014, recorded 2005, (P) 2007

BCSN xxxix (Oct 2007) p.16, *CI* xii/2 (Nov 2008) p.70

BRUCE SIMONDS

SIMb 1

*Spotlight on Keyboard

Kuhnau: Partita in G;[a] J. S. Bach: Prelude and Fugue in C;[b] Ravel: Ondine (excerpt)[b]

[a]Anon German (Belle Skinner Collection No.9), [b]Christian Gotthelf Hoffman 1784 (1)

LP Vox DL 362, 1955

LUDGER SINGER

SIN 1

Mediterra Nova (72')

Singer: Platz des himmlichen Flieders, Flamenco techno, Lusitanisches Tagebuch, Fashion, Gaze and Pyre, Sketches of Rain, Tanz der Wampentiere, Die Zen Gebote, Mediterra Nova, New Derek-tions for Clavichord, Hans Dampf in San Alberto, Make Five, Monitor aus, Herr Pastor trifft Herrn Schneider, Schon vorbei, Touch my Hall, Lämse (Bonus Blues)

Ludger Singer [c.1980, flügelförmiges clavichord]

CD Luxaries LUX 34000/3, recorded 1995-7, (P) 1997

SIN 2

*Syntopia **(62')***

[Trio Delight: Albrecht Maurer (violin), Meike Herzig (recorder, fujara), Ludger Singer (clavichord, didgeridoo)]

Ludger Singer [c.1980, flügelförmiges clavichord]

CD Classical Music Network CMN 001, recorded 2000, (P) 2001

DENIS SMALLEY

SMA 1

*Smalley: Chanson de Geste [with Carol Plantamura (voice/percussion), Denis Smalley (voice) and Douglas Docherty (percussion assistant)]

LP UEA 81063, recorded 1979

Gram (Jun 1982) p.53

JOHANN SONNLEITNER and STEFAN MÜLLER

SON 1

J. S. Bach, Die Kunst der Fuge

J. S. Bach: Die Kunst der Fuge BWV1080

Michael Scheer after Johann Heinrich Silbermann

2 CD Contrapunctus, recorded 2008/9

BCSN (Jun 2012) p.23

MARTIN SOUTER

SOU 1

Music for William Morris (71')

Gibbons: Fantasia of 4 Parts, Ground, Fantasia

Arnold Dolmetsch 1897

CD Isis CD020, (P) 1996

SOU 1a

C Isis MC020 [f/SOU 1]

SOU 2

    The Fitzwilliam Virginal Book (67')

    Philips: Pavana Philipi

    Arnold Dolmetsch 1897

    CD Classical Communications CCLCD006, recorded 1999, (P) 1999

SOU 2a

    The Fitzwilliam Virginal Book (131')

    2 CD Gift of Music CCL CD229, (P) 2006 [r/SOU 2]

SOU 3

    Music for the Six Wives of Henry VIII

    Henry VIII: Four pieces

    Anon, German c.1820 (Bate Collection, Oxford)

    CD The Gift of Music, CCL CDG1010, (P) 2002

SOU 3a

    Flower of Chivalry

    Henry VIII: Consorts IV, V, XVI

    CD The Gift of Music CCL CDG1117, (P) 2005 [r/SOU 4]

SOU 4

    Great Music from the Court of Henry VIII

    CD Classical Communications CDG1148, (P) 2006

MIKLÓS SPÁNYI

SPA 1

Johann Sebastian Bach: Inventionen & Sinfonien (58')

J. S. Bach: 15 Two-part Inventions BWV772-786, 15 Three-part Sinfonias BWV787-801

Joris Potvlieghe 1993 after mid-18th century North German models

CD PHI CD 95004, recorded 1994

BCSN v (Jun 1996) p.17, *ICD* p.12

SPA 2

Clavichord recital (65')

Mozart: Rondo in D K485, Rondo in a K511; Haydn: Sonata in E Hob.XVI:31, Arietta and Variations No.1 in Eb Hob.XVII:3; C. P. E. Bach: Rondo in E H265; Beethoven: Rondo in G Op.51/2

Joris Potvlieghe 1993 after Gottfried Joseph Horn 1785

CD PHI CD 95005, recorded 1994

BCSN v (Jun 1996) p.17, *ICD* p.12

SPA 3

C. P. E. Bach: The Solo Keyboard Music I: Prussian Sonatas I (76')

C. P. E. Bach: Sonata in a H4, Prussian Sonatas Nos.1-4 H24-27

Joris Potvlieghe 1993 after Saxon models c.1770

CD BIS CD-878, recorded 1997, (P) 1998

Tangents v (Fall 1998), p.5, *CI* ii/2 (Nov 1998) p.60, *BBCMM* (Aug 1998) p.81, *Con* (Dec 1998), *CCD* (Apr 2000) p.86, *ICD* p.12

SPA 4

C. P. E. Bach: The Solo Keyboard Music II: Prussian Sonatas II (73')

C. P. E. Bach: Prussian Sonatas Nos.5-6 H28-29, Sonatas in e H13, in C H17, in Bb H18

Joris Potvlieghe 1993 after Saxon models c.1770

CD BIS CD-879, recorded 1997, (P) 1998

CI iii/1 (May 1999) p.27, *PGCD 1999* p.36, *CCD* (Apr 2000) p.86, *ICD* p.12

SPA 5

C. P. E. Bach: The Solo Keyboard Music III: Early Sonatinas and Sonatas (80')

C. P. E. Bach: Sonata in d H5, 6 Sonatinas H7-12, Sonata in Eb H16

Joris Potvlieghe 1993 after Saxon models c.1770

CD BIS CD-882, recorded 1997, (P) 1999

CI iii/1 (May 1999) p.27, *PGCD 1999* p.36, *CCD* (Apr 2000) p.86, *ICD* p.12

SPA 6

C. P. E. Bach: The Solo Keyboard Music IV: Six Early Sonatas from 1731-1740 (79')

C. P. E. Bach: Sonatas in Bb H2, in G H20, in g H21, in F H3, in A H19, in G H15

Thomas Steiner 1991 after Christian Gottlob Hubert 1772

CD BIS CD-963, recorded 1998, (P) 1999

EMR lviii (Mar 2000) p.20, *CI* iv/1 (May 2000) p.27, *CCD* (Apr 2000) p.86, *PGCDY 2000/1* p.9, *ICD* p.12

SPA 7

Klänge de Nacht (78')

Kirnberger: Flute Sonata in G,[a] Sonata in D, Musicalischer Circul; Müthel: Flute Sonata in D,[a] Tempo di Minuetto con Variazioni [[a]with Benedek Csalog, flute]

Johann Augustin Straube 1787

CD Raum Klang RK 9804, recorded 1997, (P) 2000

EMR (Jun 2001) p.21, *BCSN* (June 2001) p.23, *CI* v/2 (Nov 2001) p.57

SPA 8

C. P. E. Bach: The Solo Keyboard Music V: Leichte Sonaten I (73')

C. P. E. Bach: Sonatas in Bb H116, in G H119, in C H162, in Bb H180, in a H181

Thomas Steiner 1991 after Christian Gottlob Hubert 1772

CD BIS CD-964, recorded 1998, (P) 2000

IRR (Oct 2000) p.81, *CI* iv/2 (Nov 2000) p.55, *ICD* p.12, *Gram* (Nov 2000) p.87

SPA 8a

*A Journey around C. P. E. Bach

C. P. E. Bach: Sonata in G H119

CD BIS CD- 311506, (P) 2004 [r/SPA 8]

SPA 9

C. P. E. Bach: The Solo Keyboard Music VI: Leichte Sonaten II (77')

C. P. E. Bach: Sonatas in g H118, in C H120, in C H163, in b H182, in F H183

Thomas Steiner 1991 after Christian Gottlob Hubert 1772

CD BIS CD-978, recorded 1998, (P) 2001

ICD p.12, *EMR* (May 2001) p.22, *CI* vi/1 (Nov 2002) p.57

SPA 10

C. P. E. Bach: The Solo Keyboard Music VII: Sonatas from 1748-49

C. P. E. Bach: Sonatas in F H55, in G H56, in d H57, in C H59, in a H61

Thomas Steiner 1991 after Christian Gottlob Hubert 1772

CD BIS CD-1086, recorded 1999, (P) 2001

BCSN (Jun 2002) p.24, *CI* vii/1 (May 2003) p.24

SPA 11

C. P. E. Bach: The Solo Keyboard Music VIII: Sonatas and Petites pièces I (69')

C. P. E. Bach: Sonatas in Eb H78; in E H117; Petites pièces H79-82, H109-13

Thomas Steiner 1991 after Christian Gottlob Hubert 1772

CD BIS CD-1087, recorded 1999, (P) 2002

EMR (Oct 2002) p.16, *BCSN* (Feb 2003) p.21, *CI* vii/1 (May 2003) p.24

SPA 12

C. P. E. Bach: The Solo Keyboard Music IX: Damensonaten (73')

C. P. E. Bach: Sonatas in F H204, in C H205, in d H184, in Bb H206, in D H185, in A H207

Thomas Steiner 1991 after Christian Gottlob Hubert 1772

CD BIS CD-1088, recorded 1999, (P) 2002

EMR (April 2003) p.20, (Oct 2003) p.25, *IRR* (May 2003) p.50

SPA 13

C. P. E. Bach: The Solo Keyboard Music X: Suite in E minor and Sonatas from 1749-52 (70')

C. P. E. Bach: Sonatas in F H58, in G H64, in D H67, in g H68, Suite in e H66

Joris Potvlieghe 1999 after Gottfried Joseph Horn 1785

CD BIS CD-1189, recorded 2000, (P) 2003

CI viii/1 (May 2004) p.30

SPA 14

C. P. E. Bach: The Solo Keyboard Music, Vol.12: Sonatas and Petites pièces 2 (66')

C. P. E. Bach: Sonatas in b H132, in e H106, in a H131, Petites pièces H89-95

Joris Potvlieghe 1999 after Gottfried Joseph Horn 1785

CD BIS CD-1198, recorded 2000, (P) 2004

CI ix/1 (May 2005) p.29

SPA 15

*Johann Gottfried Eckard: Complete Works for Keyboard (149')

Eckard: Sonatas in Bb Op.1/1, in g Op.1/2, in F Op.1/3, in E Op.2/2

Joris Potvlieghe 1999 after Gottfried Joseph Horn 1785

2 CD Hungaroton HCD 32313-14, recorded 2004, (P) 2004

BCSN (Oct 2005) p.17, *CI* ix/2 (Nov 2005) p.52

SPA 16

Johann Sebastian.Bach: A flauto traverso (66')

J. S. Bach: Flute Sonatas in e BWV1034, in E BWV1035 [with Benedek Csalog, flute]

Joris Potvlieghe 2002 after c.1770 Saxon model

CD Ramée RAM 0404, recorded 2005, (P) 2005

CI x/1 (May 2006) p.27

SPA 17

C. P. E. Bach: The Solo Keyboard Music, 14: Sonatas from 1763 and Dances (65')C. P. E. Bach: Sonatas in A H174, in e H176, in Bb H175, Alla Polaccas in C H215, in D H217, Menuets in C H159, in Eb H171, in D H214, Polonaise in Eb H172

Joris Potvlieghe 1999 after Gottfried Joseph Horn 1785

CD BIS CD-1329, recorded 2000, (P) 2005

BCSN (June 2006) p.15

SPA 18

*C. P. E. Bach: Concertos & Solo Keyboard Music, XV (141')

C. P. E. Bach: Petites pièces H96-98, 108, 114, 122-25, 301-302, 685/5, Sonatas in a H173, in d H105

Joris Potvlieghe 1999 after Gottfried Joseph Horn 1785

2 CD BIS CD-1422, recorded 2003, (P) 2006

BCSN xxxviii (Jun 2007) p.12, *CI* xiii/1 (May 2009) p.28

SPA 19

C. P. E. Bach: Württemberg Sonatas I, XVI (66')

C. P. E. Bach: Württemberg Sonatas Nos.1-3 H30-31, H33

Joris Potvlieghe 1999 after Gottfried Joseph Horn 1785

CD BIS CD-1423, recorded 2003, (P) 2006

BCSN xxxix (Oct 2007) p.16

SPA 20

C. P. E. Bach: Württemberg Sonatas II, XVII

C. P. E. Bach: Württemberg Sonatas Nos.2-4 H 32, H34, H36

Joris Potvlieghe 1999 after Gottfried Joseph Horn 1785

CD BIS CD-1423, recorded 2003, (P) 2007

BCSN xl (Feb 2008) p.18

SPA 21

C. P. E. Bach: The Solo Keyboard Music, 20: *Sonatas from 1760-66* (81')

C. P. E. Bach: Sonatas in Bb H152, in D H177, in g H210, in C H178, in Bb H212

Joris Potvlieghe 1999 after Gottfried Joseph Horn 1785

CD BIS CD-1623 recorded 2007, (P) 2009

BCSN (Oct 2010)

SPA 22

C. P. E. Bach: The Solo Keyboard Music, 21 (79')

C. P. E. Bach: Six Sonatas with varied reprises H136-9, H126, H140

Joris Potvlieghe 1999 after Gottfried Joseph Horn 1785

CD BIS CD-1624, (P) 2010

BCSN (Jun 2011) p.21

SPA 23

    C. P. E. Bach: The Solo Keyboard Music, 22: Probestücke (68')

    C. P. E. Bach: Probestücke Sonatas H70-75

    Joris Potvlieghe 1999 after Gottfried Joseph Horn 1785

    CD BIS CD-1762, recorded 2008, (P) 2011

    BCSN (Jun 2011) p.21

SPA 24

    C. P. E. Bach: The Solo Keyboard Music, 23: Sonatas from 1750-58 and other pieces (64')

    C. P. E. Bach: Sonatas in G H63, in G H77, in c H121, in A H135, Clavierstück für die rechte oder linke hand allein H241, Fantasias in d H224, in G H223, in D H160, Fugue in d H99, Solfeggios in A H222, in Eb H221, in c H220

    Joris Potvlieghe 1999 after Gottfried Joseph Horn 1785

    CD BIS CD-1763, recorded 2008, (P) 2011

    BCSN (Jun 2012) p.18

SPA 25

    C. P. E. Bach: The Solo Keyboard Music, 24: Sonatas from 1740-44 (72')

    C. P. E. Bach: Sonatas in D H22, in d H38, in E H39, in b H32.5

    Joris Potvlieghe 2010 after Saxon originals

    CD BIS CD-1764, recorded 2011, (P) 2011

    BCSN (Oct 2012) p.27

SPA 26

    C. P. E. Bach: The Solo Keyboard Music, 25: Sonatas from 1740-47 (79')

C. P. E. Bach: Sonatas in D H42, in G H23, in f H40, in F H52, in C H41

Joris Potvlieghe 2010 after Saxon originals

CD BIS CD-1764, recorded 2011, (P) 2012

BCSN (Oct 2012) p.27

SPA 27

C. P. E. Bach: The solo keyboard music, vol.26 (80')

C. P. E. Bach: Fortsetzung Sonatas No.1 in C H150, No.1 in C H156, No.2 in Bb H151, No.3 in c H127 (with embellished versions)

Joris Potvlieghe 1999 after Gottfried Joseph Horn 1785

CD BIS BIS-2040, recorded 2012, (P) 2013

BCSN (Jun 2014) p.21

SPA 28

C. P. E. Bach: The solo keyboard music, vol.27 (74')

C. P. E. Bach: Fortsetzung Sonatas No.1 in C H157, No.4 in C H128, No.5 in F H141, No.6 in g H62, No.6 in g H62 (with embellished versions)

Joris Potvlieghe 1999 after Gottfried Joseph Horn 1785

CD BIS BIS-2043, recorded 2012, (P) 2013

BCSN (Jun 2014) p.21

SPA 29

C. P. E. Bach: The solo keyboard music, 28: 'Zweyte Fortsetzung' Sonatas Nos 1-3 (74')

C. P. E. Bach: Zweyte Fortsetzung Sonatas Nos.1-3 H50, H142,

H158, Sonatas in F H240, in c H209

Joris Potvlieghe 1999 after Gottfried Joseph Horn 1785

CD BIS BIS-2045, recorded 2013, (P) 2014

BCSN (Jun 2015) p.13

SPA 30

C. P. E. Bach: The solo keyboard music, vol.29 (76')

C. P. E. Bach: Zweyte Fortsetzung Sonatas No.4 in f# H37, No.5 in E H163, No.6 in e H129, Sonatas in C H248, in c H298

Joris Potvlieghe 1999 after Gottfried Joseph Horn 1785

CD BIS BIS-2046, recorded 2013, (P) 2014

BCSN (Jun 2015) p.13

SPA 31

C. P. E. Bach: The solo keyboard music, vol.30 (75')

C. P. E. Bach: Kurze und leichte clavierstücke, H193-203, H228-238, 6 Leichte clavier-stückgen, H249-254, 6 Sonatine nuove, H292-297, 4 Keyboard pieces, H255-258, 4 Keyboard pieces, H327-330, Rondo in e Wq.66, 'Abschied von meinem Silbermannischen Claviere'

Thomas Steiner 1991 after Hubert 1772

CD BIS BIS-2125, recorded 2014, (P) 2015

BCSN (Feb 2016) p.30

SPA 32

C. P. E. Bach: The solo keyboard music, 31: 'Für Kenner und Liebhaber' Sonatas from Collections 1 & 2 (73')

C. P. E. Bach: Sonatas No.1 in C H244, No.2 in F H130, No.3 in b H245, No.5 in F H243, Sonatas No.1 in G H246, No.2 in F

H269, No.3 in A H270

Thomas Steiner 1991 after Hubert 1772

CD BIS BIS-2131, recorded 2014, (P) 2016

BCSN (Jun 2017) p.23

JOEL SPEERSTRA
[see also ULRIKA DAVIDSSON]

SPE 1

J. S. Bach: Six Trio Sonatas BWV525-530

John Barnes and Joel Speerstra 1995 after Johann David Gerstenberg 1760

CD [forthcoming]

JAAP SPIGT

SPI 1

Klinkende schoonheid iut vroeger veewen: Jaap Spight bespeelt instrumenten uit het Haags Gemeentemuseum

C. P. E. Bach: Les Folies d'Espagne H263

Anon, first half of 18th century

LP EMI 5C 063-24317

JERMAINE SPROSSE

SPR 1

Friedrich Wilhelm Rust, Der Clavierpoet: Keyboard Works (76')

Rust: Sonatas in g, in C

Thomas Steiner 1991 after Carl Gottlob Hubert 1772

CD Deutsche Harmonia Mundi 889853692972, recorded 2016, (P) 2017

BCSN (Oct 2017), p.20

LI STADELMANN

STA 1

J. S. Bach: 15 Two-part Inventions BWV772-786, 15 Three-part Sinfonias BWV787-801

LP Mercury MG 15019, 1951

STA 2

Alte Musik aus vier Jahrhunderten

C. P. E. Bach: Adagio sostenuto (from Sonata No.2 in Bb H71)

Christian Gottlob Hubert 1782

LP Deutsches Museum 0654070, [c.1977]

MARTIN STADTFELD

STAa 1

Was bedeutet eigentlich 'wohltemperiert'?

J. S. Bach: *Das wohltemperierte Klavier* (excerpts)

CD Sony Classical 88697375742, recorded 2008, (P) 2008

EINAR STEEN-NØKLEBERG

STE 1

Norsk Barokk og Galanterier

Berlin: Adagio, Menuet in a; Lindemann: Polonaise, Lagrimoso

Anon 5-octave North German (Ringve Museum)

LP Norsk Kulturrads Klassikerserie NKF 30 019, (P) 1976

STE 2

Grieg Piano Music Vol.5: Norwegian Melodies Nos. 1 to 63 (66')

Grieg: Norwegian Melodies No.4, 'Aagots Fjeldsang', No.26, 'Ro, ro te fiskesjœr, No.49, 'Ifjor gœtt'eg Geitinn', No.61, 'Den sidste Laurdags Kvelden'

CD Naxos 8.553391, recorded 1994, (P) 1995

CCD (Jun 1996) p.67, *Gram* (May 1996) p.81

STE 3

Grieg Piano Music Vol.6: Norwegian Melodies Nos. 64-117 (61')

Grieg: Norwegian Melodies No.82, 'Eg gjœtte Tulla', No.89, 'Stev (Aa vil du hava meg til aa kveda', No.96, 'Springdans fra Tin'

CD Naxos 8.553392, recorded 1994, (P) 1995

CCD (Jun 1996) p.67, *Gram* (May 1996) p.81

STE 4

Grieg Piano Music Vol.7: Norwegian Melodies Nos. 118-152 (47')

Grieg: Norwegian Melodies No.123, 'Langebergs Laat'n', No.137, 'Je teente paa Kjelstad ifjor', No.144, 'Mine Lœngsler'

CD Naxos 8.553393, recorded 1994, (P) 1995

CCD (Jun 1996) p.67, *Gram* (May 1996) p.81

BENJAMIN-JOSEPH STEENS

STEa 1

    J. S. Bach. Goldberg Variations (78')

    J. S. Bach: Goldberg Variations BWV988

    Joris Potvlieghe 1987

    CD Evil Penguin EPRC 007, recorded 2009, (P) 2010

    BCSN (Feb 2011) p.24

STEa 2

    *Bach and sons (64')

    J. C. F. Bach: Sonata in C;[a] C. P. E. Bach: Fantasia in C H291, Sonata in C H515;[a] attrib J. S. Bach: Flute sonatas in g BWV1020,[a] in Eb BWV1031;[a] J. S. Bach: Prelude, Fugue and Allegro in Eb BWV998; W. F. Bach: Sonata No.6 in a: Poco allegro [[a]with Jacques-Antoine Bresch (baroque flute)]

    Joris Potvlieghe 2010, Saxon style

    CD Evil Penguin Records Classic EPRC 011, recorded 2011 (P) 2011

    BCSN (Oct 2012) p.23

SIGRUN STEPHAN

STEb 1

    Deutsche Claviermusik

    C. P. E. Bach: Abschied vom Silbermannschen Clavier, Fantasias in F (Book 5), C (Book 6); Grotthuß: Freude über den Empfang des Silbermannschen Claviers

    Sander Ruys 2010 after attrib Johann Heinrich Silbermann

c.1775

CD Caterva Musica ECN 14.41, recorded 2014, (P) 2014

STEb 2

Kinship (73')

J. S. Bach: Prelude in c BWV999,[a] Capriccio sopra la lontananza del suo fratro dilettissimo BWV992,[a] Prelude and Fugue in G BWV884;[a] W. F. Bach/J. S. Bach: Prelude in C BWV924a;[b] W. F. Bach: Fantasia in a F23,[b] Polonaise in e;[b] C. P. E. Bach: Württemberg Sonata No.1 in a H30;[b] Reincken: Suite in G;[a] Müthel: Sonata No.1 in F[b]

[a]Sander Ruys [2010] after attrib Johann Heinrich Silbermann c.1775, [b]Martin Kather 2015 after Christian Gottlob Friederici 1765

CD Challenge Classics CC72764, recorded 2017, (P) 2017

BCSN (Jun 2018) p.13, *CI* (May 2018) p.27

DANIEL STICKAN (and organ) [with Uwe Steinmitz, saxophone]

STI 1

*Where roots grow (59')

Stickan: Where roots grow; Steinmitz: New flower; Bach arr Steinmitz: Ich steh an deiner Krippen hier; Trad arr Stickan: The water is wide; Isaac/Schulz arr Stickan: Monwald

Dietrich Hein 2015 after Späth & Schmahl

CD Edition Jazz aus Kirchen EJK 9, recorded 2016, (P) 2017

SATORU SUNAHARA

SUN 1

Mamoru Fujieda: Patterns of Plants, a clavier collection
Mamoru Fujieda: Patterns of Plants
Akihiko Yamanobe
CD Milestone art works MAM-0001

HANS KNUT SVEEN

SVE 1

*Platti: Six Flute Sonatas, Op.3 (79')
Platti: Flute sonata in A, Op. 3/4 [with Paul Wählberg (flute)]
[Joel Katzman 2005, after Anon 1700]
CD Naxos 8.570282, recorded 2005, (P) 2007

SVE 2

Siwan
[with Amina Alaoui and Barokksolistene]
CD ECM 2042, rec 2007/8, (P) 2009

DOROTHY SWAINSON

SWA 1

*J. S. Bach: Prelude in Bb BWV866 (from *Das Wohltemperierte Klavier* Book 1) (excerpt)
BBC Sound Archives 15568 (July 1950)

SWA 2

> *The History of Music in Sound, Volume VI: The Growth of Instrumental Music (1630-1750)*
>
> J. S. Bach: Prelude and Fugue in g BWV861 (from *Das Wohltemperierte Klavier* Book 1)
>
> Dolmetsch
>
> 12 12" 78 The Gramophone Company HMS 57-68

SWA 2a

> 12" 78 The Gramophone Company HMS 59 (side 6) [r/SWA 2]

SWA 2b

> LP HMV HMS 59, 1954
>
> *RG* (1955) p.886

SWA 2b

> LP HMV HLP14 [r/SWA 2]

SWA 2d

> LP RCA Victor LM-6031 [USA/SWA 2]

SWA 3

> *The History of Music in Sound, Volume VII*
>
> C. P. E. Bach: Fantasia in c H75iii
>
> Dolmetsch
>
> LP HMV HMS 81, 1957

SWA 3a

    LP HMV HLP 19 [r/SWA 3]

SWA 3b

    LP RCA Victor LM-6137 [USA/SWA 3]

SWA 4

Rameau: Le Rappel des Oiseaux,[a] Musette en Rondeau;[a] Dandrieu: La Lyre d'Orphée;[a] Couperin: Les Barricades Mystèrieuses (from Ordre N.6),[a] Le Carillon de Cythère (from Ordre No.14),[a] Les Bergeries (from Ordre No.6);[a] Scarlatti: Sonata in d K9;[a] J. S. Bach: Preludes and Fugues No. 1 in C BWV846,[c] No.2 in c BWV847,[c] No.5 in D BWV850,[b] No.13 in F# BWV858[b] (from *Das Wohltemperierte Klavier* Book 1)

Dolmetsch

LP Dolmetsch Foundation DRLP1, recorded [a]1952 and 1954, [b]1954, [c]1956

PETER SYKES

SYK 1

Johann Sebastian Bach: Preludes, Fantasies & Fugues (60')

Bach: Prelude, Fugue and Allegro BWV998, Fantasia on a rondo in c BWV918, Prelude and Fugue after Albinoni BWV923/951, Fantasia and Fugue in a BWV904, Chromatic Fantasia and Fugue in d BWV903

Johann Christoph Georg Schiedmayer 1789

CD Raven OAR-959, recorded 2012, (P) 2014

BCSN (Feb 2015) p.27, *CI* (Nov 2015) p.62

JAN VACLAV SYKORA

SYKa 1

Musical Instruments in the development of Czech Instrumental Music
Anon: Suite of dances
13 LP Supraphon SUA10378, (P) 1962

GYÖNGYVÉR SZILVÁSSY

SZI 1

Hungarian Baroque Songs & Dances (44')

Anon: Lepus intra sata quiescit, Messias iam venit (from Codex Kájoni 1664) [with Collegium Musicum, Budapest]

LP Hungaroton, (P) 1982

SZI 1a

CD Hungaroton White Label HRC 183 [1991 r/SZI 1]

LUIGI FERDINANDO TAGLIAVINI

TAG 1 [also VES 1]

Il vibrar dell'aria - A Walk through the Tagliavini Collection of Early Musical Instruments in San Colombano (160')

DVD Passacaille/Musurgia BV 1064, (P) 2019

WILLEM RETZE TALSMA

TAL 1

Klangführer durch die Sammlung alter Musikinstrumente
Pachelbel: Arietta
Anon, German c.1700
2 CD Kunsthistoriches Museum Wien 516 537-2, recorded c.1993

GENZO TAKEHISA

TAK 1

The Realms of Keyboard Music Vol.3
CD ALM Records, ALCD-1017

TAK 2

Sefauchi's farewell: Airs for harpsichord
Philip Tyre after Christian Gottlob Hubert 1787
CD Aeolian Records AEO-501, rec 1991, (P) 1991

LYNDON JOHANN TAYLOR

TAY 1

Clavichord Demonstration

J. S. Bach: French Suite No.1 in d BWV812,[a] Allemande, Courante, Sarabande, Anglaise, Menuet I (from French Suite No.3 in b BWV814),[a] Allemande, Gavotte (from French Suite No.5 in g BWV815),[a] Prelude in C BWV846 (from *Das*

Wohltemperirte Clavier Book 1);[a] Improvisation;[a] Demonstration;[b] Allemande, Courante (from J. S. Bach: French Suite No.1 in d BWV812);[acde] Improvisations;[f] Clavichord Jungle [with Brad Southard (electric guitar) and Blake Edwards (percussion)];[b] Pendulum [with Hunter Moore (electric guitar)][b]

Lyndon Johann Taylor ([a]cembal d'amour after Gottfried Silbermann, [b]electric clavichord, [c]after Christian Gottlob Hubert c.1775, [d]after Christoph Georg Schmahl, [e]after Johann Jacob Donat 1700, [f]fretted clavichord)

C [private], [1998]

ARMIN THALHEIM

THA 1

Edition Carl Philipp Emanuel Bach Volume 10: Clavichord Sonatas (61')

C. P. E. Bach: 6 Sonatas H70-75

Johann Augustin Straube 1787

CD Capriccio 10 017, recorded 1987, (P) 1988

Gram (Oct 1988) p.583, *EM* xvi (1988) p.587, *PGCD 1990* p.18

THA 1a

LP Capriccio C27 156 [f/THA 1]

THA 1b

C Capriccio CC27 156 [f/THA 1]

THA 1c

LP Eterna 725181 [V/THA 1a]

THA 1d

    CD Berlin Classics BER 9198 [USA/THA 1]

THA 1e

    CD Berlin Classics 0091982 [Germany/THA 1]

THA 1f

    Historische Tasteninstrumente aus dem Musikinstrumenten-Museum der Universität Leipzig (65')

    C. P. E. Bach: Fantasia in c H75iii

    Johann Augustin Straube 1787

    CD VKJK 9501, recorded 1994, (P) 1995 [see also WINFRIED SCHRAMMEK]

ALEXANDRE THARAUD

THA 1

    L'Oiseau innumérable

    Pécou: L'Oiseau innumérable

    Anthony Sidey 1995 after 18th century German

    CD Harmonia Mundi HMC 901974, recorded 2007, (P) 2008

WALTER THOENE

THO 1

    *J. S. Bach: Minuets in F BWVAnh 113, in Bb BWVAnh 118, in d BWVAnh 132, Polonaise in g BWVAnh 119 (from Anna Magdalena Bach Book)

Hieronymus Albrecht Hass 1728

LP Odeon 80978, 1970

MICHAEL THOMAS

THOa 1

    Froberger: Variations, Suite; Dandrieu; Böhm; Lully

    [BBC Broadcast]

THOa 2

    [Elizabethan Music]

    [BBC Broadcast]

THOa 3

    C. P. E. Bach

    Johann Nicolas Deckert 1792

    [BBC Broadcast 1960s]

THOa 4

    Seixas, Weckmann and Böhm

    Anon [Mirrey Collection], Johann Nicolas Deckert 1792

    [BBC Broadcast 1960s]

THOa 5

    Anon: Packington's Pound; Farnaby: The Old Spagnoletta, Galliard in a; Byrd: The Carman's Whistle; Gibbons: Galliard in a

    [BBC Broadcast c.1962]

THOa 6

Works for Clavichord and Harpsichord

Anthony Scott: Adagio;[a] Robert Still: Suite; Anthony Scott: Prelude and Fugue;[a] Lennox Berkeley: Prelude and Fugue Op.55/3; Eugene Goossens: Forlane and Toccata [[a]with Mary Verney, clavichord]

[mono 10" 33rpm] record Society RSX 16

THOa 7

*[Illustrated talk on the clavichord]

Hieronymus Albrecht Hass 1744 (2)

BBC Sound Archives T29158 (1963) [BBC Broadcast 1964]

THOa 8

*[Illustrated talk on the clavichord]

Hieronymus Albrecht Hass 1744 (2)

BBC Sound Archives T29159 (1964) [BBC Broadcast 1964]

THOa 9

J. S. Bach: Fantasia and Fugue in a, Chromatic Fantasia and Fugue in d BWV903

[BBC Broadcast 1964]

THOa 10

An Anthology of Elizabethan & Restoration Vocal Music

Morley: It was a Lover and his Lass; Byrd: Ye Sacred Muses [with John Whitworth, countertenor]

[Michael Thomas]

LP Saga STXID 5222

1964

THOa 10a

LP Saga XID 5222 [m/THOa 10]

THO 11

An Anthology of Elizabethan Keyboard Musick

Byrd: Rowland; John Mundy: Mundy's Joy; Farnaby: A Mask

Michael Thomas

LP Saga Pan 6202 [stereo], (P) 1966

THOa 11a

LP Saga Pan 6202 [mono], (P) 1966 [m/THOa 11]

THOa 12

Pachelbel: Aria No.4 (from *Hexachordum Apollonis*); J. S. Bach: Suite in a BWV818; Couperin: Ordre No.25 in C

[BBC Broadcast c.1966-1967]

THOa 13

Historic Harpsichord and Clavichords

Froberger: Suite in G, 'Auf die Mayerin', Lamento (from Suite No.30);[a] Buxtehude: Allemande, Suite d'Amour;[b] Ritter: Suite and Fugue in f#[b]

[a]Michael Thomas, [b]Johann Nicolas Deckert 1792

LP Oryx 1725 [stereo], [1967]

Gram (Jan 1968), *Gram* (May 1970)

THOa 13a

    LP Oryx 1725 [v/THOa 13]

THOa 14

    *Anon: Italian Pavane; Froberger: Suite No.9 in a; Reincken: Ballet and Variations; Seixas: Toccata in f; Weckman: Suite in a

    Anon [Mirrey Collection]

    LP BBC Sound Archives LP 31312 (December 1967)

THOa 15

    Bach on the Clavichord

    J. S. Bach: Suite in F BWV823, Aria Variata BWV989, Chromatic Fantasia and Fugue in d BWV903; attrib J. S. Bach: Fantasias in c BWV921, in g BWV917

    Michael Thomas

    LP Oryx *Bach Collector's Series* BACH 1231

    Gram (Aug 1970)

THOa 15a

    *Bach's Keyboard Instruments

    J. S. Bach: Aria Variata BWV989; attrib J. S. Bach: Fantasias in c BWV921, in g BWV917

    CD Oryx Baroque Music Club BACH 740 [r/THOa 15]

THOa 16

    Michael Thomas plays music by Johann Josef Fux (1660-1741) on a Clavichord built by himself

    Fux: Harpeggio and Fugue in G E114, Partita in g E117, Sonata

No.7; Capriccio in g K404; Ciacona in D K403

Michael Thomas 1953

LP Oryx 1716, recorded 1964/5, (P) 1973

Gram (Apr 1973), *RR* (Aug 1973) p.64

THOa 16a

LP Oryx 716 [USA/THOa 16]

THOa 16b

*Johann Josef Fux: Chamber Music (74')

Fux: Harpeggio and Fugue in G E114, Sonata No.7; Ciacona in D K403

CD Oryx Baroque Music Club BMC 28 [2002 r/THOa 16]

THOa 17

*L'Art des Instruments d'Amour

J. S. Bach: French Suite No.2 in c BWV813, Prelude and Fugue in b BWV893 (from *Das Wohltemperierte Klavier* Book 2 BWV870-893)

Michael Thomas (Cembal d'amour)

Arion AR 36369A, recorded 1976, (P) 1977

THOa 18

Weckmann: Suites and other Keyboard Works

Weckmann: Suites in d, in a, in e, in c, in b, Variations on 'Die Lieblichen Blicke', Toccata

Michael Thomas after Christian Gotthelf Hoffman 1784 (2)

C Merlin Performance PERC 86071, recorded 1984, (P) 1984

THOa 19

J. S. Bach: Well Tempered Clavier, Book I

J. S. Bach: Das Wohltemperierte Klavier Book 1 BWV846-869

Michael Thomas after Christian Gotthelf Hoffman 1784 (2)

2 LP Saga Psyche PSY 4/5

Gram (Mar 1985), *MT* cxxvi (Mar 1985) p.161, *EHM* iii/8 (Apr 1985) p.165

THOa 20

J. S. Bach: Well Tempered Clavier, Book II (152')

J. S. Bach: Preludes and Fugues in C BWV870,[a] in c BWV871,[b] in C# BWV872,[c] in c# BWV873,[b] in D BWV874,[c] in d BWV875,[b] in Eb BWV876,[b] in eb BWV877,[b] in E BWV878,[c] in e BWV879,[c] in F BWV880,[b] in f BWV881,[b] in F# BWV882,[b] in f# BWV883,[c] in G BWV884,[a] in g BWV885,[c] in Ab BWV886,[b] in g# BWV887,[b] in A BWV888,[b] in a BWV889,[a] in Bb BWV890,[a] in bb BWV891,[a] in B BWV892,[a] in b BWV893[b] (from *Das Wohltemperierte Klavier* Book 2 BWV870-893)

[a]Michael Thomas 1986 [pentagonal, BB-d^3], [b]Michael Thomas 1953, [c]Gottfried Joseph Horn 1788

2 CD Alpha 290 845 A, recorded live 1987-1988

JOHN TILBURY

TIL 1

*Seaside (62')

Improvisations: Biyar 'Adas, Saqiya, Jarisha, al-Safirriya; Lely: Line; Christian Wolff arr Tilbury: Tilbury 2, Tilbury 4 [with

John Lely (electronics) and Dirar Kalash (oud)]

CD another timbre at 100, recorded 2016

COLIN TILNEY

TILa 1

Fantasien (50')

J. S. Bach: Chromatic Fantasia and Fugue in d BWV903, C. P. E. Bach: Fantasias in c H75iii, in C H291; W. F. Bach: Fantasia in d F19; C. P. E. Bach: Fantasia in C H284; Mozart: Fantasia in d K385g

Hieronymous Albrecht Hass 1742 (1)

LP Deutsche Grammophon Archiv 2533 326, recorded 1975, (P) 1976

Gram (Apr 1978) p.1750

TILa 1a

C Deutsche Grammophon Archiv 3310 326 [f/TIL 1]

TILa 1b

Carl Philipp Emanuel Bach: Odes, Psalms & Lieder (55')

C. P. E. Bach: Fantasias in c H75iii, in C H291

CD Deutsche Grammophon Archiv *Codex* 453 168-2 [r/TIL 1]

PGBCD 1998 p.1315, *PGCDY 2000/1* p.615

TILa 1c

*Codex Collection

10 CD Deutsche Grammophon Archiv *Codex* 453 161-2 [s/TIL 1b]

TILa 1d

    *[Codex Sampler] (76')

    C. P. E. Bach: Fantasia in C

    CD Deutsche Grammophon Archiv *Codex* 453 172-2 [r/TIL 1b]

TILa 2

    *J. S. Bach: Das Wohltemperierte Klavier (304')

    J. S. Bach: Das Wohltemperierte Klavier Book 1 BWV846-869

    Johann Adolph Hass 1767

    4 CD Hyperion CDA 66351/4, recorded 1988, (P) 1990

    Gram (Oct 1990) p.775, *Gram* (Mar 1991) p.1753, *ICD* p.14

TILa 2a

    **A Performer's Guide to Music of the Baroque Period*

    J. S. Bach: Prelude and Fugue in B BWV686 (from *Das Wohltemperierte Klavier* Book 1)

    CD accompanying Associated Board book, Anthony Burton (ed), *A Performer's Guide to Music of the Baroque Period* (London, 2002) [r/TIL 2]

TILa 3

    C. P. E. Bach: Fantasia in C Wq.61/6; Mozart: Fantasia in d K397; Haydn: Sonata in g Hob.XVI:44; W. F. Bach: Polonaise in e F12/10; Mozart: Suite in the style of Handel K399, Minuet in D K355; Beethoven: Variations on an original theme WoO77

    Arnold Dolmetsch [Russell Collection]

    [BBC Broadcast 1997]

TILa 4

Music for Clavichord (27')

Pachelbel: Aria prima (from *Hexachordum Apollonis*); Froberger: Ricercar No.5 (1656), Lamento (from Suite No.6); Frescobaldi: Elevation Toccata No.3 (excerpt); Dowland arr Schiedemann: Lachrimae; Kirnberger: Polonaises in F, in G

Jörg Gobeli after Anon 17th century German

CD (Private label), recorded 2002

TILa 5

C. P. E. Bach: Six Clavichord Sonatas (77')

C. P. E. Bach: 6 Sonatas for Connoisseurs and Amateurs, Book 1 (1779): H130, H186, H187, H243-245

Arnold Dolmetsch 1895 after Johann Adolph Hass

CD Doremi DDR-71146, recorded 2004, (P) 2005

CI x/2 (Nov 2006) p.59

TILa 6

J. S. Bach: The Six French Suites (123')

Bach: French Suites Nos.1-6 BVW812-817, Menuet and Sarabande (Suite in a BWV818a), Allemande and Menuets (Suite in Eb BWV819a)

Arnold Dolmetsch 1895 after Johann Adolph Hass

2 CD Music & Arts MACD-1268, recorded 2009, (P) 2012

BCSN (Jun 2013) p.24

RICHARD TROEGER

TRO 1

J. S. Bach: The Six Partitas (142')

J. S. Bach: Partitas Nos.1-6 BWV825-830

Ronald Haas 1979 after Johann Heinrich Silbermann

2 CD Lyrichord LEMS-8038, (P) 1999

ICD p.14, *BCSN* xv (Oct 1999) p.21, *CI* iii/2 (Nov 1999) p.59, *EM*, xxvii/4 (Feb 2000) p.140, *Tangents* viii (Spring 2000), p.1-3

TRO 2

J. S. Bach: The Seven Toccatas (70')

J. S. Bach: Toccatas Nos.1-7 BWV910-916

Ronald Haas 1979 after attrib Johann Heinrich Silbermann

CD Lyrichord LEMS-8041, (P) 2000

ICD p.14, *BCSN*, xv (Oct 1999) p.21, *CI* iv/2 (Nov 2000) p.56, *PGCDY 2000/1* p.20, BCSN , xviii (Oct 2000) p.17

TRO 3

J. S. Bach: Inventions, Sinfonias, Little Preludes (68')

J. S. Bach: 15 Two-part Inventions BWV772-786,[a] 15 Three-part Sinfonias BWV787-801;[b] 12 Short Preludes BWV924-930, 939-942, 999,[a] 6 Short Preludes BWV933-938[b]

Ronald Haas 1979 after three [a]Anon German fretted instruments, late 17th century/early 18th century, Ronald Haas 1986 after [b]attrib Johann Heinrich Silbermann

CD Lyrichord LEMS-8047, (P) 2000

CI v/2 (Nov 2001) p.56

TRO 4

J. S. Bach: The Art of Fugue (135')

J. S. Bach: The Art of Fugue BWV1080 [with Paulette Grundeen in Contrapunctus 12a/b],[ab] Chromatic Fantasia and Fugue BWV903,[a] Adagio in G BWV968,[a] Sonata in d BWV964,[a] Partita in E BWV1006a,[a] Fantasia in a BWV922[a]

[a]Ronald Haas 1979 after Johann Heinrich Silbermann, [b]Lyndon Taylor 1998 after attrib Gottfried Silbermann

2 CD Lyrichord LEMS-8048, (P) 2005

BCSN (Oct 2005) p.20, *CI* ix/2 (Nov 2005) p.54, *EM* xxxiv/3 (Aug 2006) p.507

MICHAEL TSALKA

TSA 1

201 Years of Grace (105')

Christian Kull: 12 Variations in C on Gubben Noak; Mozart: 6 Variations on Salve tu Domine K398, 6 Variations in A K Anh.137, Sonata in D K311; Türk: Sonatas in D HedT.99.3.b, in C HedT.99.3.4; Haydn: Sonata in Bb Hob.XVI:41

Lindholm & Soderström 1808

CD Robert Holmin Ljud & Bild RHL&B 07, rec 2009, (P) 2012

BCSN (Jun 2010) p.24

TSA 2

*Türk: Keyboard sonatas, collections I and II (157')

Türk, Collection I (1776), Sonata No.5 in a Hedt.97.1.5; Collection II (1777), Sonatas No.1 in d Hedt.98.2.1, No.5 in c Hedt.98.2.5

Johann Paul Kraemer & Sons 1804

2 CD Grand Piano GP627-28, recorded 2010 (P) 2012

BCSN (Feb 2013) p.20, CI (Nov 2013) p.54

TSA 3

*Türk: Six keyboard sonatas for connoisseurs (1789) (60')

Türk, Sonata No.2 in Eb Hedt.104.8.2

Christian Kintzing 1763

CD Grand Piano GP657, recorded 2012 (P) 2013

TSA 4

Bach: Goldberg Variations (67')

J. S. Bach, Goldberg Variations BWV988

Two instruments by Sebastian Niebler 2010, 2011 after J. C. G. Schiedmayer 1796 and late 18th German models

CD Paladino Music pmr 0032, recorded 2012 (P) 2013

CI (Nov 2013) p.53, BCSN (Feb 2014) p.20, HFP (Autumn 2014) p.35

JAROSLAV TŮMA

TUM 1

Pachelbel, Froberger: Clavichord Compositions

Pachelbel: Fugue in C, Aria Sebaldina in f, Fugue in b, Ciaccona in F; Froberger: Toccata No.16 in C, Canzona No.3 in F, Toccata No.19 in d, Fantasia No.2 in a, Canzona No.5 in G, Suite in G, 'Auf die Mayerin'

LP Supraphon 11 1008-1 131, recorded 1987

TUM 2

Johann Sebastian Bach: Inventions & Sinfonias, Duets (71')

J. S. Bach: 15 Two-part Inventions BWV772-786, 15 Three-part Sinfonias BWV787-801; 4 Duets BWV802-5

Johann Christoph Georg Schiedmayer 1789

CD Arta F1 0076-2, recorded 1996, (P) 1997

CI ii/1 (May 1998) p.27, *Tangents* vi (Summer 1999), p.4, *ICD* p.15

TUM 2a

Histoické Klavíry V Čechách a Na Morave (63')

J. S. Bach: Two-part Invention Nos. 8 in F BWV779, Three-part Sinfonias No.2 in c BWV788; Duet No.1 in e BWV802

CD [r/TUM 2], included with book by Bohulslav Čížek, *Histoické Klavíry V Čechách a Na Morave* (Prague, 2010)

TUM 3

J. S. Bach: *Das Wohltemperierte Klavier* Book 1 BWV846-869 (131')

Martin Kather 1999 after description by David Tannenberg 1760

2 CD Supraphon SU 3600-2 132, recorded 2000, (P) 2002

CI vi/1 (May 2002) p.27

TUM 4

*J. S. Bach: Goldberg Variations (154')

Martin Kather 2002 after description by David Tannenberg 1761, Martin Kather 2004 after Christian Gottlob Hubert 1787

2 CD Arta F10136, recorded 2004, (P) 2005

CI x/1 (May 2006) p.26, *EM* xxxiv/3 (Aug 2006) p.507

TUM 5

J. S. Bach: The Well-Tempered Clavichord

J. S. Bach: *Das Wohltemperierte Klavier* Book 1 BWV846-869;[a]
Das Wohltemperierte Klavier Book 2 BWV870-893[b]

[a]Martin Kather 1999 after David Tannenberg manuscript,
[b]Martin Kather 1997

4 CD Arta F10165, recorded 2000/2002, (P) 2002/2008 [2008 r/ TUM 3]

BCSN xliii (Feb 2009) p.23

TUM 6

Johann Jakob Froberger, Clavichord Fantasias (80')

Froberger: Capriccio XIII, Suites II, III, VI, Fantasia I, Canzona V; Tůma: Improvisations I-VII

Martin Kather after Anon Italian c.1600; after Hubert 1787, Martin Kather after 'German masters in the French style'

CD Arta F10184, (P) 2011

BCSN (Jun 2012) p.21, *CI* (May 2012) p.28

TUM 7

A Portrait of Clavichord (126')

Graupner: Suite in C (Ouverture, Chaconne, Entrada; J. S. Bach: French Suite No.6 in E BWV 817; C. P. E. Bach: Rondo II in c Wq.59/5, Fantasia I in F Wq.59/4; Štěpán: Sonata in Eb; Mozart: Variations on Ah, vous dirai-je, Maman K265; Howells: Lambert's Clavichord, Op. 41; J. S. Bach arr Tůma: Chaconne in d BWV1004

Johann Christoph Georg Schiedmayer, 1787

2CD, Arta F10241, recorded 2019, (P) 2019

ERICH TŮRK

TUR 1

Erich Türk la clavicordul Muzeului de Istorie din Sighişoara (65')

Bach: French Suite No.5 in G BWV816; Sweelinck: Mein junges Leben hat ein End; Anon: Suite in C (Codex Caioni); Georg Muffat: Passacaglia (Apparatus musico-organisticus); Benedetto Marcello arr Bach: Concerto in d BWV974; Philipp Caudella: Tema con variazioni

Samuel Joseph Maetz c.1800

CD Transylvantiqs TR2, recorded 2008, (P) 2009

NAOKO UEO

UEO 1

Quiet conversations (76')

C. P. E. Bach: Fantasias in A H278, in f# H300, Folies d'Espagne H263, Sonatas in Eb H16, in a H30, in G H119, Marche in D BWV Anh.122, Polonaise in g BWV Anh.123, Marche in G BWV Anh.124, Polonaise in g BWV Anh.125, Solo in Eb BWV Anh.129

Akio Obuchi 2008 after Johann Jacob Donat 1700, Akio Obuchi 2009 after Christian Gotthelf Hoffmann 1784

CD Waon WAONCD-260, recorded 2013, (P) 2014

BCSN 63 (Oct 2015) p.16

ERIK VAN BRUGGEN

VAN 1

J. S. Bach: Pedaalclavichord (51')

J. S. Bach: Praeludium in a BWV569, Trio Sonata No.1 in Eb BWV525, Prelude and Fugue in C BWV545, Fugue in G BWV577, Passacaglia in c BWV582, Fugues in d BWV539, in g BWV542

Dick Verwolf after Johann David Gerstenberg 1760

CD M.R.S. CD 9310012, recorded 1993

Tangents vi (Summer 1999), p.3, *ICD* p.8

VAN 2

Pedal Clavichords (51')

Sweelinck: Praeludium pedaliter;[a] Schiedemann: Praeambulum in G;[a] Buxtehude: Praeludium in d BuxWV140,[a] Praeludium in C BuxWV136;[a] Ritter: Sonatina;[a] J. S. Bach: Prelude and Fugue in Eb BWV552;[b] Fantasia and Fugue in c[b]

[a]Dick Verwolf 2002 after 17th-century models, [b]Dick Verwolf 1991 after Johann David Gerstenberg 1760

CD M.R.S. CD 032001-2, recorded 2003

CI ix/1 (May 2005) p.30, *EM* xxxiii/2 (May 2005) p.356

MENNO VAN DELFT

VANa 1

Johann Gottfried Müthel: 3 Sonates et 2 Ariosi et 12 Variations (110')

Müthel: Sonatas in F, in G, in C, Arioso in G, Arioso in c

Johann Adolph Hass 1763

2 CD Teknon TK 12-252, recorded 2002, (p) 2004

CI ix/2 (Nov 2005) p.55, *EM* xxxiii/2 (May 2005) p.355

VANa 2

J. S. Bach Partitas (134')

J. S. Bach: Partitas Nos.1-6 BWV825-30

Christian Gotthelf Hoffmann 1784

2 CD Resonus Classics RES10212, recorded 2016, (P) 2018

BCSN 72 (Oct 2018) p.17, *CI* xxii/2 (Nov 2018), p.62

MENNO VAN DELFT and SIEBE HENSTRA

VANa 3

Bach Edition [see also BEL 1a]

Bach: Fuga a 2 clav BWV1080xviiia, Alio modo, Fuga a 2 clav BWV1080xviiib, Canon in Hypodiatesseron BWV1080xiv (from The Art of Fugue BWV1080)

Geert Karman 1989 after Friderici 1765, Geert Karman 1989 after Johann Adolph Hass 1761, 1763

160 CD Brilliant Classics 99697, recorded 1999, (P) 2000

VANa 3a

Bach Edition, vol 92: Die Kunst der Fuge, part 2

12 CD Brilliant Classics 99372/1-12 [s/VANb 1]

ELZA VAN DER VEN

VANb 1

Telemann: Der getreue Music-Meister (271')

Haltmeier: Fantasia in D

5 LP Deutsche Grammophon Archiv SKL 943-947, recorded 1966-1967, (P) 1967

VANb 1a

4 CD Deutsche Grammophon Archiv 447 722-2 [r/VANc 1]

Gram (Apr 1996) p.98

AIMEE VAN DER WIELE

VANc 1

Messe Gaudeamus de Josquin des Prés – Les fresques musicales

LP A Charlin Disques CC 40L

NELLY VAN REE BERNARD

VANd 1

Psalteries & Clavichords designed and played by Nelly van Ree Bernard

C Eurosound, (P) 1992

VANd 2

Early Iberian Music and Sephardic Songs (70')

Anon: Ma mare me dona,[a] Albuquerque,[a] Albuquerque;[a] Encina: Pues que ya nunca nos veis;[b] Vasquez: No puedo apartarme de los amores, madre;[b] Anon: Conde Claros[b]

[a]Tangent Tetrachord by Martin Sassmann 1980, [b]Koen Vermeij 1983 after plans by Bermudo 1555

CD Eurosound Digital ES 47.166 CD

BCSN iii (Oct 1995) p.16

VANd 3

Spaanse en Portugese Claviermuziek 16e tot 20e eeuw (30')

Cabezón: Pavana con su glosa; da Cruz: Verso de 8o tom por d-sol-re; Scarlatti: Sonata in a; Seixas: Toccata in d; Soler: Sonata in D; Carvalho: Toccata in g; Mateo Albeniz: Sonata in D; Isaac Albeniz: Rumores de la Caleta; de Grignon: Ballades

Koen Vermeij 1987 after Christian Gottlob Hubert 1776

CD NvRB-71.CD, recorded 1998, (P) 1998

VANd 4

Clavichord opnames uit 1978 (48')

Anon: Pues no me quereis hablar; O glorioso Domina; Fabordon llano (from Henestrosa, *Libro de Cifra Neuva* 1557); Santa María: Fuga a 2 voces (from Santa María, *Arte de Tañer Fantasía*); van Ree Bernard: Fantasia de la misma fuga; Encina: Pues que ya nunca nos veis (from *Cancionero Musical de Palacio*); Vasquez: No puedo apartarme; Josquin, arr Palero: Kyrie; Urreda, arr Cabezón: Pange lingua; Cabezón: Pavana con su glosa (from Henestrosa, *Libro de Cifra Neuva* 1557); Josquin, arr Narváez: Canción del Emperador (from *Los seys Librso del Delphin* 1538); Sweelinck: Toccata; Batchelor: Round; Scarlatti: Sonata; Rameau: Menuet; C. P. E. Bach: Sonata

Martin Sassman 1973 after Christian Gottlob Hubert

CD NvRB-76.CD, recorded 1978, (P) 2000

VANd 5

Van Paumann tot Haydn (28')

Paumann: Mit ganczem Willen (from *Fundamentum organisandi* 1452); Dalza: Pavana (from *Intavolatura* 1508); Cabezón: Pavana con su glosa (from Henestrosa, *Libro de Cifra Neuva* 1557); Anon: A good Polish dance (from Leoffelholtz Tablature); Sweelinck: Volte; Dowland: John Smith his Alman (from *Varietie of Lute Lessons* 1610); Pasquini: Variationi; Daquin: Le coucou; Carvalho: Allegro (from Sonata in D); Haydn: Finale (from Sonata in D)

Koen Vermeij 1987 after Christian Gottlob Hubert 1776

CD NvRB-77.CD, recorded 2000, (P) 2000

VANd 6

Een middeleeuwse muziekreis

CD Muziekcentrum 'Het Diuntje', NvRB-91, recorded 1993/1998/2005, (P) 2005

GERARD VAN REENEN

VANe 1

*Domenico Scarlatti: Sonatas

Jacob Verwolf c.1976

CD [no label or date], recorded 2001, (P) 2001

JEROEN VAN VEEN (also piano, electric keyboard, clavichord, synthesizer)

VANf 1

Riley 'in C' (80')

Riley: In C

CD Brilliant Classics 95217, recorded 2015, (P) 2015

GERARD VAN VUUREN

VANg 1

Il sussurro (36')

C. P. E. Bach: Flute Sonatas in C Wq.73, in G Wq.86 [Il Sussurro, with Amanda Marwick (baroque flute)]

Klinkhamer & Partners 2006 after attrib Johann Heinrich Silbermann c.1775

CD il sussurro [no number], recorded 2009, (P) 2009

PEKKA VAPAAVUORI

VAP 1

Five Variations on the theme of Anders Wåhlström: Pekka Vapaavuori plays clavichords built by himself (60')

Froberger: Suite No.6 in C; Böhm: Suite No.7 in F; J. S. Bach: 6 Short Preludes BWV924-928, BWV930; attrib Haydn: Sonata in Bb Hob.XVI:2; C. P. E. Bach: Sonata in G H137; Böhm: Allemande (from Suite No.7 in F) [played 5 times]

5 clavichords by Pekka Vapaavuori after Anders Wåhlström 1752

CD Sibelius Academy SACD-10, recorded 1997, (P) 1998

Tangents v (Fall 1998), p.5, *ICD* p.15, *CI* iii/2 (Nov 1999), p.60

DENIS VAUGHAN

VAU 1

Bach after Midnight (59')

Attrib J. S. Bach: Musette in D BWVAnh 126, Menuet in a BWVAnh 120, Aria in d; Petzold: Menuet in G BWVAnh 114;

Attrib J. S. Bach: Menuet in c BWVAnh 121, March in D; J. S. Bach: Wer nur den lieben Gott BWV691; Attrib J. S. Bach: Menuets in G and g (from Anna Magdalena Bach Book); C. P. E. Bach: Andante (from Sonata in C H244), Allegretto (fom Sonata in b H245); J. S. Bach: Preludes in C BWV846, in F BWV881, in Ab BWV862, in E BWV854, in bb BWV867, in F BWV856, in F# BWV858, in a BWV889, in eb BWV853 (from *Das Wohltemperierte Klavier*)

Thomas Goff 1939

LP Arabesque, [c.1972]

VAU 1a

C Arabesque 9044 [1980 r/VAU 1]

MARY VERNEY

[see MICHAEL THOMAS]

TEMENUSCHKA VESSELINOVA

VES 1 [also TAG 1]

*Il vibrar dell'aria - A Walk through the Tagliavini Collection of Early Musical Instruments in San Colombano (160')

DVD Passacaille/Musurgia BV 1064, (P) 2019

MARIO VIDELA

VID 1

**Clavier-Büchlein für Anna Magdalena Bach* (77')

J. S. Bach: Menuet in G BWV841, Air in c BWV991

Eckehardt Merzdorf after Hieronymus Albrecht Hass 1740
CD Hänssler 92.135, recorded 1999, (P) 1999

VID 1a [HIL 1, LEV 1, PAY 1]

J. S. Bach 2000: The Millennium Edition
170 CD Hänssler, (P) 2000 [s/VID 1]

FINN VIDERØ

VIDa 1

Masterpieces of Music before 1750
Froberger: Suite in e
Neupert
LP Haydn Society HSL 2072, 1953

VIDa 1a

LP Haydn Society 9039 [r/VIDa 1]

HARALD VOGEL

VOG 1

...Rund um Bach, Volume 1 (66')
Attrib J. S. Bach: 8 Short Preludes and Fugues BWV553-560; J. S. Bach: Nun komm, der Heiden Heiland BWV599, Gelobet seist du, Jesu Christ BWV604 (from *Das Orgelbüchlein*), Prelude in g BWV535, Das alte Jahr vergangen ist BWV614, Jesus Christus, unser Heiland BWV626, Erschienen ist der herrliche Tag BWV629 (from *Das Orgelbüchlein*), Prelude and Fugue in e

BWV533, Wenn wir in höchsten Nöten sein BWV641, Wer nur den lieben Gott lasst walten BWV642 (from *Das Orgelbüchlein*), Fantasia in G BWV572

John Barnes and Joel Speerstra 1995 after Johann David Gerstenberg 1760

CD Organeum OC-29701, recorded 1997, (P) 1998

CI ii/2 (Nov 1998) p.60, *ICD* p.15

PETER WALDNER

WAL 1

Mozart: Sonaten & Variationen (64')

Mozart: Sonatas in a K310, in D K311, in C K545, Variations on 'Ah, vous dirai-je maman' K300c

Koen Vermeij 1994 after Christian Gottlob Hubert 1771

CD Extraplatte EX-663-2, recorded 2005

BCSN 38 (June 2007) p.15, *CI* xii/2 (Nov 2008) p.69

WAL 2

**Vergessen und wieder entdeckt: Die Blockflöte. Alte und Neue Musik 1926-1943 auf Originalinstrumenten* (76')

CD Verein der Freunde und Förderer des Musikinstrumenten-notabene, (P) 2013

WAL 3

**Ex Bibliotheca Mariaemontana*

Handel: Fugues in g HWV605, in Bb HWV607, in a HWV609

Joseph Lusser c.1820

CD Tiroler Landesmuseum MMCD13033, rec 2017, (P) 2018

WAL 4

J. S. Bach: Toccaten & Suiten am Clavichord, Vol. 1

J. S. Bach: Toccatas in d BWV913, in c BWV911,
in G BWV916, Sonata in d BWV964,
French Suite No.2 in c BWV813

Joris Potvlieghe 2018 after Jacob Adlung 1726

CD Organroxx 11, rec 2018, (P) 2019

RALF WALDNER

WALa 1

Claviermusik aus Nürnberg (76')

Staden: Allamanda varirt; Schultheiss: Suite in G

Andreas Hermert 2009 after Anon German

CD TYXart TXA 13037, recorded 2012, (P) 2013

EMR (Oct 2014) p.44, *BCSN* (Jun 2016) p.18

HEINRICH WALTHER

WALb 1

European Keyboard Music (73')

J. S.Bach: Adagio, Allegro (from Sonata in d BWV1003)

Dietrich Hein 1999 after Swedish instrument c.1730

CD Organeum Classics OGM 200035, recorded 2000, (P) 2000

DAVID WARD

[see STEVEN DEVINE]

YUKO WATAYA

WAT 1

J. S. Bach and C. P. E. Bach: Works for Clavichord (62')

J. S. Bach: Partita No.6 in e BWV830; C. P. E. Bach: Sonata in e H188, Rondo in A H276, Württemberg Sonata No.1 in a H30

Jean Tournay 1996 after mid-18th century North German unfretted originals

CD René Gailly CD87 139, recorded 1997, (P) 1998

Con (Dec 1998), *CI* iii/1 (May 1999) p.28, *ICD* p.16

WAT 2

Haydn, Early keyboard sonatas (151')

Haydn: Sonatas Hob.XVI:G1, Hob.XVI:1, 2, 4, 10-12

Jean Tournay 1994 after Johann Hieronymous Hass 1761

2 CD Pavane ADW 7486/7, recorded 2001, (P) 2003

ALEXANDER WEIMANN

WEI 1

*Telemann: Duos pour flûtes

Matthias Maute: Fantaisie I – V pour clavicorde

Eckehardt Merzdorf 1982

CD Atma ACD 2 2309, recorded 2003, (P) 2004

PETER WIDENSKY

WID 1

Il clavicordio mirable - musik bis 1635
Michael O'Brien 1984
CD [no number], (P) 2013

WID 2

Musik vor 1540
Michael O'Brien 1984
CD [no label], rec 2011

PETER WILLIAMS

[see also LUCY CAROLAN]

WIL 1

Handel: Suite in d;[a] [music by Frescobaldi[b] and Mozart[c]]
[a]Anon c.1750, [b]Anon Italian/German c.1700, [c]Johann Adolph Hass 1763 (1)
LP BBC Sound Archives LP 34630 (August 1972)

MANON-LIU WINTER

WIN 1

10. Komponistenforum Mittersill 8.–17. September 2005
2 CD Ein Klang Records Nr.018/019, rec 2005, (P) 2005

WIM WINTERS

WINa 1

Music from Bach to Beethoven (223')

Buxtehude: Suite in e; Pachelbel: Ciaconna in f; Handel: Suite in d; J. S. Bach: Two–part Inventions Nos.7-9 BWV778-780, Prelude & Fugue in E BWV854, Partita No.1 in Bb BWV825; C. P. E. Bach: Abschied von meinem Silbermannischen Claviere; J. C. Bach: Sonata in c Op.17/2; Haydn: Sonatas in Ab Hob. XVI:46, in Bb Hob.XVI:41; Mozart: Variations in F K398, Adagio in b K540, Sechs Deutsche Tänze K509; Clementi: Sonata in f# Op.26/2; Beethoven: Pathetique Sonata in c Op.13; Schubert: Gretchen Am Spinnrade; Cramer: Etudes Nos.16 in f, 18 in d, 21 in G, 24 in d; Czerny: Prelude & Fugue in G; Papazafeiropoulos: Rondo in a, Sonata in c Op.113

Joris Potvlieghe 2009 after Saxon models

3 CD Authentic Sound Records AS1601, recorded 2014-16

CI xxi/2 (Nov 2017), p.69, *BCSN* (Jun 2018) p.10

WINa 2

Johann Pachelbel: Hexachordum Apollinis 1699 (53')

Pachelbel: Hexachordum Apollinis

Joris Potvlieghe 2009 after Saxon models

CD/LP/FLAC/mp3/mp4 Authentic Sound AS001, recorded 2017-18, (P) 2018

BCSN (Summer 2019) p.17

WINa 3

Bach: Partitas

2 CD Authentic Sound Records (forthcoming)

ILTON WJUNISKI

WJU 1

Musique Ibérique au clavicorde (76')

Cabezón: Tiento del sexto tono con segunda parte;[a] Lassus arr Cabezón: Susanne un jour;[a] Cabezón: Discante sobre la pavana Italiana;[a] Correa de Arauxo: Tiento de registro entero de primero tono,[b] Tiento y discurso de segundo tono;[a] Bartolomeu de Olagué: Variedades da Xácara de 1o tom;[a] Cabanilles: Tiento lleno de primero tono,[a] Gallardas de tercero tono;[b] Mudarra: Cifras para Harpa y Organo;[b] Carreira: Canção;[b] Reis: Concertado sobre o Canto Chão de Ave Maris Stella;[a] Coelho: Susana grozada a 4 sobre a de 5;[b] Anon: [Himno a 3];[b] Coelho: Terceiro Kyrio do primero tom por C Sol Fa Ut,[a] Quarto Kyrio do mesmo tom,[a] Quinto Kyrio do mesmo tom;[a] Braga: [b]Batalha de 6º tom[b]

[a]Edwin Meier after Jacinto Ferreira 1783, [b]Edwin Meier after Anon [Portuguese?], late 18th century

CD Harmonia Mundi *Schola Cantorum Basiliensis Documenta* HMC 90 5236, recorded 1995, (P) 1997

Gram (Aug 1997) p.76, *BCSN* (Feb 1998) p.12, *Con* (Apr 1998), *CI* ii/1 (May 1998) p.27

WJU 2

*J. S. Bach: French Suites (149')

J. S. Bach: French Suites Nos.1-6 BWV812-817, Suites in a BWV818a, in Eb BWV819, in f BWV823

Thomas and Barbara Wolf 1989 after attrib Johann Heinrich Silbermann

2 CD GM recordings GM2075CD, recorded 1995-1996, (P) 2004

EM xxxiii/2 (May 2005) p.355

WJU 2

Friedrich Wilhelm Rust (212')

Rust: Sonatas in F, in g, in Eb, in G, in A, in Db, in d, in e, in G, in C, in f#, in D

Carl Gottlob Sauer 1807

3 CD Querstand VKJK 1421, recorded 2009, (P) 2017

BCSN (Oct 2017), p.20, *CI* (May 2018) p.28

JULIEN WOLFS
[see MARIE-ANNE DACHY]

ROBERT WOOLLEY

WOO 1

J. S. Bach: Prelude in b BWV869 (from *Das Wohltemperierte Klavier* Book 1), French Suite No.3 in b BWV814a, Prelude in C BWV846 (from *Das Wohltemperierte Klavier* Book 1), French Suite No.2 in c BWV813

Anon unfretted 18th century (Mirrey collection)

BBC recording (June 1985)

WOO 2

The soul's inspiration

W. F. Bach: Fantasia in c, Polonaises No.4 in d F12/4, No.3 in

D F12/3; Rust: Sonata (1792); Hassler: Sonata in a (1776); G. Benda: Sonata No.4 in F

Derek Adlam after Johann Adolph Hass

BBC recording (14 January 1988)

WOO 3

Valente: Lo Ballo dell' Intorcia, Bascia Flammignia, Fantasia in Mode I; Cabezón: Pavana Italiana, Canto del Caballero, Gallarda Milanesa; Valente: La Romanesca

Eric Dodson

BBC Broadcast [late 1980s]

CHRISTIANE WUYTS

WUY 1

Quatre instruments à clavier

Froberger: Suite in F

K. & M. Kaufmann 1970 after Anon 17th century

LP Alpha DB 175, (P) [1977]

YASUHIRO YAMADA

YAM 1

J. S. Bach: 15 Two-part Inventions BWV772-786, 15 Three-part Sinfonias BWV787-801; C. P. E. Bach: Sonata in d H208

Eckehardt Merzdorf 1997 after attrib Johann Heinrich Silbermann

CD BAGK 1012, recorded live 8 November 1998, (P) 1999

YAM 2

    J. S. Bach: French Suites Nos.1-6 BWV812-817; C. P. E. Bach: Sonata in F H243

    Eckehardt Merzdorf 1997 after Johann Heinrich Silbermann

    CD BAGK 1013, recorded live 18 July 1999, (P) 1999

TOSHIYUKI YAMANA

YAMa 1

    Haydn Keyboard works (71')

    Haydn: Sonatas in c Hob.XVI/20, in Eb Hob.XVI/52

    CD ALM Records ALCD-9138, rec 2012, (P) 2014

EILIF ZACHARIASSEN

ZAC 1

    Værker af Georg Böhm, J. S. Bach og C.Ph.E.Bach

    Böhm: Suite No.11 in a; J. S. Bach: Chromatic Fantasia in d BWV903; C. P. E. Bach: Variations on 'Les Folies d'Espagne' H263, Fantasias in f# H300, in C H291, Rondo in e H272, 'Abschied von meinem Silbermannischen Claviere'

    Adlam Burnett 1976 after Johann Adolph Hass 1763

    C Songbird/Carsten Lehn [no number], (P) 1981

    EM xi (1983) pp.143, 407, *OY* xiv (1983) p.141

JEAN-CLAUDE ZEHNDER

ZEH 1

Deutsche Clavier-Musik um 1700

Pachelbel: Variations on 'Werde munter, mein Gemüte'; Reincken: Fugue in g

Berhardt Edskes

LP Vox Humana VH 30-654, recorded 1978-79

OY xiii (1982) p.169

UNKNOWN

UNK 1

Mozart, "Ich hätte München Ehre gemacht" (89')

Michael Eder 2004, after Johann Andreas Stein 1762

DVD edel 0169838 ERE, recorded 2005, (P) 2006

UNK 2

Three films (202')

Chronicle of Anna Magdalena Bach

2 DVD new wave films 009, 1967

Notes

[1] There is in fact a slightly earlier film, available on <http://www.youtube.com/watch?v=RDcvJRuBAfI>, in which one can see – but not hear – Dolmetsch playing the clavichord in 1928. The earliest harpsichord recording, by Violet Gordon Woodhouse, dates from 1920.

[2] For more on Chopin on the clavichord, see McElwain (2010) and Knights (2019).

[3] Artists include Tori Amos, Donald Amram, Roger Ball, Billy Bang, Barry Beckett, Xentos 'Fray' Bentos, Jackson Berkey, Nick Bicat, Vincent-Marie Bouvot, Jeff Bova, David Briggs, Brandon Bush, Mike Cavanagh, Robert Collins, Andrew Cronshaw, Ronnie Cuber, Chip Davis, Bo Donaldsen, Thomas Darnal, Vic Emerson, Magne Furuholmen, Albhy Galuten, Lisa Gerrard, Kevin Gilbert, Andrew Gold, Robbie Gordon, Friedrich Gulda, Herbie Hancock, Elisabeth Harnik, Donald Hepburn, Michael Hepburn, Oscar Jan Hoogland, Robert Julian Horky, Clayton Ivey, Katharina Klement, Ned Lagin, Howard Levy, Dexter de Los Angeles, Hans Lüdemann, Bobby Lyle, Simon Jeffes, Booker T. Jones, Sharona Joshua, Katharina Klement, Paul MacCartney, Beryl Marriott, Roberto Scarpa Meylougan, Kerry Minnear, Fonce Mizell, Don Moye, John Musselwhite, Triona Ní Dhomhnaill, Josef Novotny, Michaél O'Súilleabháin, Sonny Ovalle, Barry Phillips, Don Preston, Michael Robinson, Joe Sample, Derek Shulman, Guy Sigsworth, Ludger Singer, Derek Smith, Alison Statton, Rick Steff, Mayumi Tachibana, Lyndon Johann Taylor, Mike Willox, Manon Liu Winter, Bernie Worell, Davod Yazbek and Zazie.

[4] For details of Dart's recordings with L'Oiseau-Lyre, see Davidson 1994.

[5] For details concerning the making of this recording, see Kirkpatrick 1981 and 1984.

Composer Index

Adam	CLE 1
Agrell	DEV 1, GRU 4
Agricola	CLE 4
Åhlström	GRU 4
Albero	BRA 6
Albato	CAN 1
I. Albeniz	VANd 3
M. Albeniz	VANd 3
Alberto	CLE 4
Alvarado	BRA 10
Antico	BAL 1
ap Rhys	SIM 4
Arcadelt	CLE 4
Aston	BRA 2, BRA 11
Attaingnant	BRA 1, CLE 4, KAN 3, LEH 1
C. P. E. Bach	ADL 1, AVE 1, AVE 2, BEG 1, BEL 3, BEN 1, BEN 2, BEN 4, BEN 5, BEN 6, BOD 3, BRA 7, CAR 1, CHAa 1, BRE 1, BRO 1, CAL 2, CER 2, CHAa 3, CRE 1, CUI 1, CUI 2, CUI 3, CUI 4, CUM 1, DUP 1, DYS 2, GAT 1, GAT 2, GEO 1, GIL 1, GOE 1, GOV 1, GRU 2, GRU 3, GUM 1, HAD 2, HAM 1, HOG 3, HOG 7, HOL 2, ISE 1, ISE 2, JON 1, JUN 3, KAN 1, KIP 2, KIP 6, KLA 1, LAL 1, LEC 1, LEH 1, LEO 2, LEO 3, MCG 1, MIY

	1, MUL 1, NEU 2, NEU 4, NEU 5, NIC 1, NIC 2, POL 1, ROB 1, SCHc 1, SEL 1, SIM 1, SPA 2, SPA 3, SPA 4, SPA 5, SPA 6, SPA 8, SPA 9, SPA 10, SPA 11, SPA 12, SPA 13, SPA 14, SPA 17, SPA 18, SPA 19, SPA 20, SPA 21, SPA 22, SPA 23, SPA 24, SPA 25, SPA 26, SPA 27, SPA 28, SPA 29, SPA 30, SPA 31, SPA 32, SPI 1, STA 2, STEa 1, STEb 1, STEb 2, TUM 6, SWA 3, THA 1, THOa 3, TILa 1, TILa 3, TILa 5, UEO 1, VANg 1, WINa 1, VANd 4, VAP 1, VAU 1, WAT 1, YAM 1, YAM 2, ZAC 1
J. C. Bach	ALE 1, BRA 13, BRE 1, ISE 1, KRU 1, WINa 1
J. C. F. Bach	JUN 3, KIT 2, ROB 1, STEa 2
J. S. Bach	ADL 1, ADL 2, AVE 1, AVE 2, BAU 1, BEL 1, BEL 4, BER 2, BER 3, BOD 1, BOD 3, BOG 1, BRE 1, BUR 1, CHO 1, CHO 2, COO 1, CRA 1, CRE 5, CRO 1, CUI 1, DAR 3, DAR 6, DEC 1, DEL 1, DOL 1, DOL 2, ELL 1, FAR 1, FEN 1, FRO 1, GEO 1, GHI 1, GRU 1, GRU 3, GUG 2, GUL 1, GUL 5, HAK 2, HAM 1, HAMa 1, HAR 1, HENa 2, HIL 1, HIL 2, HIL 3, HIL 4, HOG 4, HOG 7, HOL 1, HOS 1, HUN 1, ISE 1, JOH 1, JON 1, JUN 1, KAN 2, KAR 1, KIP 1, KIP 6, KIP 7, KIR 1, KIR 2, KIR 3, KIR 4, KIR 5, KIR 6, KIR 7, KIT 1, KIT 3, KLA 1, KRU 1, LAL 1, LEC 1, LEH 1, LEH 2, LEO 3, LEV 1, LEV 2, LEV 3, LEV 4, MCE 1, MCG 1, MON 1, MON 2, MORa 2, MUL 1, NEU 1, NEW 1, OTS 1, PAY 1,

	PAY 2, PAY 3, PER 2, PFL 1, PIC 1, RIN 1, RIN 2, RIN 4, RIN 6, RIN 7, SAX 2, SEL 1, SEV 1, SIMb 1, SON 1, SPA 1, SPA 16, SPR 1, STA 1, STAa 1, STEa 1, STEa 2, STEb 2, SWA 1, SWA 2, SWA 4, SYK 1, TAY 1, THO 1, THOa 9, THOa 12, THOa 15, THOa 17, THOa 19, THOa 20, TILa 1, TILa 2, TILa 6, TRO 1, TRO 2, TRO 3, TRO 4, TSA 4, TUM 6, TUM 2, TUM 3, TUM 4, TUM 5, TUR 1, VAN 1, VAN 2, VANa 2, VANa 3, VAP 1, VAU 1, VID 1, VID 2, VOG 1, WAL 4, WALa 1, WAT 1, WINa 1, WJU 2, WOO 1, YAM 1, YAM 2, ZAC 1
W. F. Bach	AVE 2, BARa 1, BEN 5, BEN 6, BUR 2, GEO 1, GOR 1, GOR 2, GRA 1, HOG 7, JUN 3, KAN 1, LEO 3, NEU 3, ROB 1, SIM 2, SIM 5, STEa 1, STEb 2, TILa 1, WOO 2
Bacharach	CRO 1
Baldi	BRA 5
Banchieri	LEH 1
Baptista	CAL 1, CAN 1
Bark	GRU 4
Bartók	CRA 1, KRU 1, LEH 1
Batchelor	VANd 4
Bebelaar	BEB 1
Beethoven	CRO 1, DRE 1, MCE 1, MCE 2, SCHa 1, SPA 2, TILa 3, WINa 1
G. Benda	KLAa 1, WOO 2
Bendusi	CHA 1, KAN 3

Berkeley	THOa 6
Berlin	MOS 1, STE 1
Binchois	SIM 4
Blanco	BRA 13, KAS 4
Blondeau	CHAa 4
Boësset	CHAa 4
Blow	AVE 1
Böhm	ISE 2, KIP 6, LEH 1, LEH 2, LEO 4, THOa 4, VAP 1, ZAC 1
Bonelli	DELb 1
Braga	WJU 1
Broege	BRO 1
Brubeck	DES 1
Brumel	SIM 4
Buchner	CLE 4, SIM 4
Bull	BRA 2, RAM 6
Buttstedt	KRA 1
Buxtehude	ROBa 1, SIM 2, THOa 13, WINa 1
Byrd	BRA 1, BRA 11, DOL 3, MORa 1, ROBa 1, SAX 1, THOa 5, THOa 10, THOa 11
Cabanilles	CHA 1, WJU 1
A. de Cabezón	BAC 1, BEN 1, BEN 6, BRA 2, BRA 11, CAN 1, CLE 3, CLE 4, KAN 3, KAS 1, KAS 3, LEC 1, MAR 1, VANd 3, VANd 4, VANd 5, WJU 1, WOO 3
H. de Cabezón	CHA 1
J. de Cabezón	MAR 1

Caccini	LEH 1
Camp	CAM 1
Carpenter	NAS 1
Carreira	BRA 10, BRA 11, WJU 1
Carvalho	BRA 5, SIM 1, VANd 3
Caudella	TUR 1
Cavazzoni	BRA 11
Cellier	CHAa 4
Chambonnières	CHAa 4
Chopin	MCE 1
Clay	KWA 1
Clemens	CLE 4
Clementi	WINa 1
Coelho	BRA 2, BRA 10, WJU 1
Collin	GRU 4
Constanz	CLE 4
Correa	KAS 3, WJU 1
Costeley	CHAa 4
L. Couperin	CHAa 4
F. Couperin	LAL 1, RIN 1, SWA 4, THOa 12
Cramer	WINa 1
Crecquillon	CLE 3, SIM 4
Crees	CRE 2, CRE 4, CRE 6
Croft	AVE 1, DAR 1, DAR 2, DAR 6, DAR 7
Crossan	CRO 1
Czerny	WINa 1

Da Cruz	BRA 10, VANd 3
Dalza	CHA 1, KAN 3, VANd 5
Dandrieu	AVE 1, SWA 4
Daquin	VANd 5
de Araújo	BRA 10
Debussy	LEH 1
de La Barre	CHAa 4
de Olagué	WJU 1
De Paiva	BRA 10
de Soto	CLE 4
Dickinson	DIC 1, DIC 2, DIC 3
Dietrich	CLE 1
Dodgson	CUC 1, PER 1
D'Orléans	CHAa 4
Dowland	TILa 4, VANd 5
Drusina	CLE 4
Dubut	GRU 4
Dufay	KITa 1
Dünki	DUN 1, DUN 2
Eckard	SPA 15
Egiguren	BRA 6
Elköf	PERa 1
Ellington	DIC 1, DIC 2, DIC 3
Encina	VANd 2, VANd 4
Etxeberria	BRA 6

Facoli	KAN 3, MIE 1
Falla	BRE 1
G. Farnaby	AVE 1, BOL 1, CRE 1, CRE 3, HEN 1, THOa 5, THOa 11
R. Farnaby	CRE 1
C. F. Fasch	PER 4
Feliciano	LEH 2
Févin	CHAa 4
Finck	SAR 1
Fischer	BEN 1, HAM 1, HENa 2, OTS 1, SCHd 1
Frescobaldi	CHA 1, CHL 1, HAA 1, KAS 2, LOR 1, TILa 4, WIL 1
Froberger	BEN 1, BEN 5, BEN 6, BOG 1, BOG 3, CHAa 5, KIT 3, DAR 4, DAR 7, GOE 1, HENa 2, ISE 2, KIP 3, LEC 1, PER 2, RAM 1, RAM 2, RIN 3, THOa 1, THOa 13, THOa 14, TILa 4, TUM 1, TUM 5, VAP 1, VIDa 1, WUY 1
Fuenllana	LEC 1
Fujieda	SUN 1
Fux	MCE 2, THOa 16
A. Gabrieli	ACE 1, BRA 2, BRA 11, CHA 1, SIM 4
Galuppi	GIG 1
Gardane	CHAa 4, SCHc 2
Gascogne	BRA 2, BRA 11
Gaultier	KAN 3, LEH 1
Gerlach	GER 1, GER 2
Gershwin	PET 1

Gesualdo	LEOa 1
Gibbons	CRE 1, LEH 1, LEH 2, SOU 1, SOU 3, THOa 5
Gigault	CHAa 4
Goossens	THOa 6
Graupner	AVE 2, TUM 6
Grenzer	GRU 4
Grieter	CLE 1
Grieg	STE 2, STE 3, STE 4
Grotthuss	ADL 1, BEN 1, BEN 3, BEN 6, CRE 1, STEb 1
Gulda	GUL 1
Gulda/Goethe/Anders	GUL 1
Handel	GUM 1, HOG 5, WAL 3, WIL 1, WINa 1
Harrison	BRO 1
Hasse	KIP 6, MCG 1
Hässler	BENa 1, DEV 2, KLA 1, SIM 2, WOO 2
Haydn	ADL 3, BARa 1, BEG 2, BEN 5, BEN 6, CER 1, CER 2, CRA 1, CUR 1, DAV 1, ELL 1, GEO 1, HAD 1, HAK 1, KIP 3, KRU 1, LAU 1, MIY 1, NEU 4, NEU 6, SCHb 1, SCHe 1, SPA 2, TILa 3, VANd 5, VAP 1, WAT 2, WINa 1, YAMa 1
Henestrosa	CLE 4, VANd 4
Henry VIII	CRE 3, SOU 4
Hoddinott	DIC 1, DIC 3
Hofhaimer	CLE 1, CLE 4, EDL 1, HENa 2, SAR 1, SCH 1, SIM 4

Hollander	CLE 4
Horn	LEH 2
Hovhaness	BRO 1
Howells	AVE 1, BRO 1, CRA 1, DYS 1, DYS 2, PER 3, TUM 6
Hurley	HUR 1
Huys	HUY 1
Isaac	CLE 4, EDL 1
Jachet	CLE 4
Jacinto	CAL 1
Jarrett	JAR 1
Jobartheh/Lüdemann	LUD 2
Johnsen	MCE 2
Josquin	CLE 1, CLE 3, MAR 1, VANd 1, VANd 4
Kapsberger	MOR 1
Kerll	BIL 1, BIL 2
Kindermann	KAN 3
Kirnberger	AVE 2, SPA 7, TILa 4
Kolberg	BRA 1, BEU 1
Korhonen	KOR 1, KOR 2, KOR 3, KOR 4
Kosinski	BRO 1
Kotter	BRA 1, CHA 1, CLE 4, HENa 2
Kreiger	HOG 5, OTS 1
Kuhnau	BEN 4, BOD 2, BUT 1, HENa 2, KIP 2, SCHc 1, SIM 2, SIMb 1

Kull	TSA 1
Lagerfeldt	GRU 4
Larrañaga	BRA 6
Lassus	CLE 4, WJU 1
Lèbegue	CHAa 4
Legrand/Evans	LEH 1
Legrant	MIE 1
Lehmann	LEH 1, LEH 2
Lely	TIL 1
Lennon & McCartney	LAUa 1
Ligeti	MCE 1
Lindemann	STE 1
Lislevand	MOR 1
Lithander	MCE 1, MCE 2
Locatelli	CIO 1
Lüdemann	LUD 1
Lully	RIN 8
Luther	LEH 2
Madre de Deus	BRA 5, BRA 10
Madsen	MAD 1
Marcello	DEC 1, TUR 1
Mattheson	GUM 1
Maute	WEI 1
Megnier	CHAa 4
Mendelssohn	GOR 1

Merulo	SIM 4
Milan	BRA 1, CHA 1, LEH 1
Morley	THOa 10
Mouton	CLE 3, CLE 4
Mozart	BEL 2, BIR 1, BRA 9, CARa 1, CER 2, DEC 1, DEC 2, DEC 3, DEC 4, DEC 5, DEC 6, DYS 3, GOY 1, HAM 1, HOG 6, IRV 1, KIP 3, KRU 1, NEU 5, PEN 1, RAM 7, RAM 8, RAM 9, RAM 10, RAM 11, RAM 12, RAM 13, RAM 14, RAM 16, SCHa 2, SIM 1, SPA 2, TILa 1, TILa 3, TSA 1, TUM 6, WAL 1, WIL 1, WINa 1
Mudarra	LEH 1, WJU 1
Muffat	AVE 2, CRE 1, RAM 3, TUR 1
J. Mundy	THOa 11
Müthel	CER 2, GOY 2, SIM 2, SPA 7, STEb 2, VANa 1
Narváez	BRA 11, CHA 1, JEA 1, KAN 3, LEC 1, LEH 1
Nassarre	BRA 2
Neefe	DRE 1
Newman	LEH 1
Newsidler	BRA 1, LEH 1
Noermiger	KAN 3
Obrecht	BRA 2
Olivares	BRA 13, KAS 4
Oxinaga	BRA 6

Pachelbel	CRE 1, CRE 3, KIP 2, LEH 1, LEH 2, MAD 1, PAY 4, TAL 1, THOa 12, TILa 4, TUM 1, WINa 1, WINa 2, ZEH 1
Palero	CAN 1, CLE 4
Papazafeiropoulos	WINa 1
Paradisi	PAR 3
Pasquini	BEN 3, DELb 1, KAS 2, VANd 5
Pass	LEH 1
Pasterwiz	CLE 2
Pathie	CLE 4
Paumann	BRA 1, BEU 1, CHA 1, HOG 2, KAN 3, LEH 1, VANd 5
Pécou	THA 1
Peerson	AVE 1, CRE 1, CRE 3
Pellegrini	DELb 1
Pergolesi	RIN 8
Perrichon	BEN 1, BEN 6
Persichetti	BRO 1
Persson	PERa 1
Petzold	KIP 6
Phalèse	CLE 4
Philips	RAM 5, RAM 15, SIM 4, SOU 2
Picchi	KAN 3
Picco	PIC 1
Pinel	CHAa 4
Platti	MOL 1, SVE 1
Pleyel	GRU 4
Polak	BEN 6

Purcell	AVE 1, CRE 1, DAR 2, DAR 6
Quantz	GIA 1
Racquet	CHAa 4
Raes	DEM 1
Rameau	RIN 3, SWA 4, VANd 4
Ravel	SIMb 1
Reichart	KOC 1
Reincken	GUM 1, HIL 3, HIL 4, STEb 2, THOa 14, ZEH 1
Reis	WJU 1
Reger	MUL 2
Ridout	DIC 2, DIC 3
Riley	VANf 1
Ritter	LEO 3, THOa 13, VAN 2
Roman	GRU 4, PAR 1, PAR 2
Rota	CRO 1
Rust	SPR 1, WJU 2, WOO 2
Saint-Saëns	MCE 1
Santo Elias	BRA 5
Sandrin	CHA 1, CLE 4
Santa Maria	HOG 1, KAN 3, LEH 1, VANd 4
Sanz	BRE 1
Sarti	CAT 1
Scarlatti	AVE 1, BOG 2, COL 1, CRE 1, KIP 5, RIN 5, SWA 4, VANd 3, VANd 4, VANe 1

Scheidt	LEH 1, LEH 2
Schiedemann	VAN 2
Schoenberg	LEH 1
Schubert	WINa 1
Schultheiss	WALa 1
Schwartz	LEH 1
Scott	THOa 6
Scronx	CHAa 4
Seixas	BRA 4, BRA 8, CAL 1, FER 1, FER 2, THOa 4, THOa 14, VANd 3
Senfl	CHA 1, CLE 1, CLE 4
Sermisy	CLE 4
Seterholm	GRU 4
Shuster	DYS 3
Singer	SIN 1, SIN 2
Smalley	SMA 1
Smit	LAU 1
Soderini	DELb 1
Soler	BRA 3, BRA 12
Sostoa	BRA 6
Soto	KAS 1
Speth	JEA 1
Staden	WALa 1
Štěpán	TUM 6
Steinmitz	STI 1
Stickan	STI 1
Still	THOa 6

Stölzel	KIP 6
Sweelinck	CHA 1, CHAa 4, ELL 1, KRU 1, RAM 4, TUR 1, VAN 2, VANd 4, VANd 5
Swensson	GRU 4
Tallis	LEH 1
Telemann	AVE 2, GUM 1, PER 2, PFL 1, VANb 1
Trabaci	BEN 6
Türk	DAC 1, KLA 1, KOC 1, TSA 1, TSA 2, TSA 3, SIM 2
Ureda	CLE 4, VANd 4
Usher	GRE 1
Valente	BRA 1, BRA 2, BRA 11, KAN 3, WOO 3
Vanhal	AUZ 1
van Ree Bernard	VANd 4
Vasquez	VANd 2, VANd 4
Vecchi	CLE 4
Verdelot	CLE 3, CLE 4
Victoria	LEH 1
Vivaldi	DEC 1. GHI 1
Vulpius	LEH 2
Wagenseil	BEN 6
Walther	LEH 1, LEH 2
Webern	MCE 1
Weck	CLE 4, KAN 3

Weckmann	GUM 1, HENa 1, THOa 4, THOa 14, THOa 18
Wolf	SIM 3
Wolff	TIL 1
Woodman	BRO 1
Zachow	HOG 5, KRU 1
Zipoli	AVE 1, CRE 3
Zorn	DRU 1
Zwingli	CLE 1
Anon	BEN 1, BEN 6, BRA 1, BRA 11, BROa 1, CHAa 1, CHAa 3, CHAa 4, CAN 1, CLE 1, CLE 4, CRA 1, CRE 1, CRE 3, DAN 1, DAR 1, DYS 3, ERD 1, ERD 2, ERD 3, GOR 1, GOR 2, GRU 4, HENa 2, IMM 1, JOS 1, KAN 1, KAN 3, KIT 3, LEH 1, LEH 2, LES 1, SCHd 2, SIM 4, SYKa 1, THOa 5, THOa 14, TUR 1, VANd 2, VANd 4, VANd 5, WJU 1

Historic Instruments Index

Anon, unfretted (Clemencic Collection)	CLE 3, CLE 4
Anon [Germany c.1600] (German Nat. Museum)	BAC 1
Anon, Germany (Belle Skinner No.9)	SIMb 1
Anon, Germany, late 17th century	CHAa 1, HUN 1
Anon, Germany c.1700	TAL 1
Anon, Germany c.1730	BEU 1
Anon, [Iberia] second half 17th century	BRA 10
Anon, Italy/Germany c.1700	WIL 1
Anon, first half of 18th century	SPI 1
Anon. c.1620 (Edinburgh)	ACK 1, KIT 3, THOa 4, THOa 14
Anon, c.1750	WIL 1
Anon, early 18th century	KOR 1
Anon, early 18th century (Brussels M1619)	HENa 2
Anon [Spain, 17th century]	BROa 1
Anon [Portugal, second half of 17th century]	BRA 11
Anon [?Portugal, early 18th century]	FER 1
Anon, 18th century	HAR 1
Anon, unfretted 18th century (Edinburgh)	KIT 3, WOO 1
Anon, South Germany 18th century	NEU 5
Anon, five-octave North Germany (Ringve)	STE 1
Anon [ex-Nannerl Mozart]	BIR 1
Anon, 2nd half of the 18th century [ex-Mozart]	BIR 2, HOG 6
Johann Jacob Bodechtel c.1790	HOG 4, HOG 5

Franz Joseph Bouthillier 1790	ERD 1-3
Bartolomeo Cristofori 1719	DEL 1
Johann Nicolas Deckert 1792	THOa 3, THOa 4, THOa 13
Johann Jacob Donat 1700	BER 2, SCHc 1
Johann Christoph Fleischer 1728	MOS 1
Barthold Fritz 1751	AVE 2, JON 1
Johann Christian Gerlach 1769	GUM 1
Johann Heinrich Gräbner 1761	HOG 5
Hieronymus Albrecht Hass 1728	THO 1
Hieronymus Albrecht Hass 1742 (1)	CHO 1, CHO 2, GUM 1, GUM 2, TILa 1
Hieronymus Albrecht Hass 1744 (2)	THOa 7, THOa 8
Johann Adolph Hass 1761 (4)	HOG 3, HOG 4, HOG 5, HOG 6, HOG 7
Johann Adolph Hass 1763 (1)	CARa 1, IRV 1, KIT 1, VANa 1, WIL 1
Johann Adolph Hass 1763 (2)	HOG 7
Johann Adolph Hass 1767	NIC 1-2, TILa 2
Egidius Heyne 1781	BRA 9
Christian Gotthelf Hoffman 1784 (1)	CER 2, HAMa 1, SIMb 1, VANa 2
Gottfried Joseph Horn 1788	KLAa 1, THOa 20
Christian Gottlob Hubert 1756	HAM 1
Christian Gottlob Hubert 1772	JUN 1
Christian Gottlob Hubert 1782	GIL 1, STA 2

Christian Gottlob Hubert 1784 (4)	KIT 2
Christian Kitzing 1763	TSA 3
Mathias Petter Kraft 1806	KOR 1
John Paul Krämer & Sons 1804	TSA 2
Pehr Lindholm 1780	BEN 5, BEN 6, SIM 5
Pehr Lindholm 1785 (3)	BARa 1, BARa 2
Pehr Lindholm 1788	MIY 1
Pehr Lindholm 1791	KOR 2
Pehr Lindholm 1792	PAR 2
Pehr Lindholm 1799	GRU 4
Pehr Lindholm & H. J. Söderström 1806	DEV 1, DEVa 2, LAUa 1
Pehr Lindholm & H. J. Soderström 1808	KOR 3, KOR 4, MAL 1, MCE 1, PERa 1, TSA 1
Pehr Lundborg 1775	SIM 1
Pehr Lundborg 1778	PERa 1
Joseph Lusser c.1820	WAL 3
Samuel Joseph Maetz c.1800	TUR 1
Domenicus Pisaurensis 1543	SCHc 2
Gottlieb Rosenau 1778	GRU 4
Carl Gottlob Sauer 1807	KOC 1, WJU 2
Johann Christoph Georg Schiedmayer 1787 (3)	TUM 6
Johann Christoph Georg Schiedmayer 1789	SYK 1, TUM 2
Johann Christoph Georg Schiedmayer 1791	HOG 6
Johann Christoph Georg Schiedmayer 1796	BEN 3, BEN 5
J. & P. Schiedmayer (Stuttgart Collection)	KAS 1
attrib Carl Christian Schmahl, late 18th century	JUN 3, NEU 1,

	NEU 3, NEU 4, NEU 5, NEU 6
Georg Friedrich Schmahl 1807	BUR 1, BUR 2
attrib Gottfried Silbermann	SCHc 1
attrib Johann Heinrich Silbermann c.1775	CHO 2, HAK 1
Philip Jacob Specken 1743	KOR 1
Johann Augustin Straube 1787	SPA 7, THA 1
[attrib] Onesto Tosi 1568	BEN 3, BRA 2
Peter Weidtman 1724	DOP 1
Georg Woytzig 1688	KOR 1

Bibliography

Frances Bedford, *Harpsichord & Clavichord Music of the Twentieth Century* (Berkeley, 1993)

Tom Beghin, *The Virtual Haydn: Paradox of a Twenty-First-Century Keyboardist* (Chicago, 2015)

Lothar Bemmann, *Clavichord-Musik on CD*
<http://members.aol.com/dcsdd>

_____ 'Northheimer Clavichord Nachrichten', in *Clavichord International* (1997-)

_____ 'The Clavichord in Films', in B. Brauchli, J. Wardman and A. Galazzo (eds), *De Clavicordio* VII (Magnano, 2006), pp.249-57

Donald Boalch, ed Charles Mould, *Makers of the Harpsichord and Clavichord* (Oxford, 3/1995)

Bernard Brauchli, *The Clavichord* (Cambridge, 1998)

Trevor Croucher, *Early Music Discography* (London, 1981)

Jim Davidson, *Lyrebird Rising: Louise Hanson-Dyer of L'Oiseau-Lyre 1884-1962* (Carlton, Victoria, 1994)

Kenneth Dommett, 'Discography of Keyboard Works of C. P. E. Bach', in Philip Barford, *The Keyboard Music of C. P. E. Bach* (London, 1965), pp.179-180

Jessica Douglas-Hume, *Violet: The Life and Loves of Violet Gordon Woodhouse* (London, 1996)

Martin Elste, *Modern Harpsichord Music: A Discography* (Westport, CT, 1995)

Hugh Gough, 'Sound recording at Jesses', *The Consort* iv (Jul 1937), p.18-19

Ralph Kirkpatrick, 'On Playing the Clavichord', *Early Music*, ix (Jul 1981), pp.293-305

_____ *Interpreting Bach's Well-Tempered Clavier* (Yale, 1984)

Francis Knights, 'A Clavichord Discography', *Music Review*, li/3 (Aug 1990), pp.221-233

_____ 'C. P. E. Bach and the Clavichord: Interpretations on Record', [illustrated talk given in London, Nov 1998]

_____ 'The Clavichord on CD', *International Clavichord Directory* (London 2001, 2/2005)

_____ *Clavichord Discography - A comprehensive listing of audio and visual recordings of the clavichord 1931-2009* (Cambridge, 2009)

_____ 'On-line resources for the keyboard player', *British Clavichord Society Newsletter*, lvi (Jun 2013), pp.34-36

_____ 'Exploring Chopin on the clavichord', *Tangents* xlv (Oct 2019), pp.1-4

Anna Maria McElwain, *A Clavichordist's View of the Chopin Preludes* (Sibelius Academy, 2010)

William Parsons, 'Early Keyboard Bibliography-Discography', *Early Keyboard Journal*, viii (1990)

Denis Vaughan, 'Taping the Sounds of Quiet', *High Fidelity/Musical America*, xxii (Aug 1972), p.50

Lavern Wagner, 'The Clavichord Today', *Periodical of the Illinois State Music Teachers Association* vi/1, (1968) pp.20-38 and vii/1, pp.1-16

Dick Wahlberg, 'Revisiting the 1928 Art of recording the Clavichord: Comparisons and Comment', *Tangents*, xvii (Fall 2004), pp.

Judith Wardman (ed), *International Clavichord Directory* (London, 2001, 2/2005)

Michael Zapf, 'How do you record the clavichord?', *Clavichord International*, i/1 (May 1997), p.21

_____ 'The Amplification and Recording of Clavichords: A Symposium in Basel', *British Clavichord Society Newsletter* xvii (Jun 2000), pp.17-19

www.ingramcontent.com/pod-product-compliance
Lightning Source LLC
Chambersburg PA
CBHW080409230426
43662CB00016B/2358